My Philips
AIRFRYER
COOKBOOK

100 Fun & Tasty Recipes for Healthier Families

By

Rebecca Dunlea

My Philips AirFryer Cookbook
100 Fun & Tasty Recipes for Healthier Families
Copyright © 2016 Rebecca Dunlea

Royal Philips of the Netherlands is a leading health technology company focused on improving people's health and enabling better outcomes across the health continuum from healthy living and prevention, to diagnosis, treatment and home care. Philips leverages advanced technology and deep clinical and consumer insights to deliver integrated solutions. The company is a leader in diagnostic imaging, image-guided therapy, patient monitoring and health informatics, as well as in consumer health and home care. Rebecca Dunlea is not affiliated with Royal Philips.

Cover photo credits: resnick_joshua1 / Depositphotos.com
stillfx / Depositphotos.com

Back cover: bhofack2 / Depositphotos.com, studioM / Depositphotos.com, nito103 / Depositphotos.com, bhofack2 / Depositphotos.com

Interior photos: All interior photos are from Depositphotos.com
Hannamariah p. 7, bhofack2 p. 14, dolphfynlow p. 49, lenyvavsha p. 82, bhofack2 p. 168, nito103 p. 209

Legal Disclaimer

TABLE OF CONTENTS

INTRODUCTION

The Air Frying Revolution

Throughout time, a central contradiction has plagued the common home cook: the more butter, oil, and grease you add to most any dish, the more delicious it will taste...and the unhealthier it will be. That's due mainly to simple chemistry. Oil is a highly efficient conductor of heat, which means that it can quickly heat foods uniformly across their surface areas. That fast all over cooking is what achieves the golden brown outer crunch that makes fried food so delicious. But without using high quantities of artery clogging oil, chefs simply had no tools to achieve the same effect.

For those of us who want food to nourish our bodies as well as our flavor palates, this is less than ideal. I've spent years trying to strike the optimal trade off in my recipes between taste and nutrition. Like most cooks, I've also spent more dollars than I care to recount on various brands of convection oven and other gadgets, in an effort to achieve the all-over heat circulation that makes deep fried foods so tasty. None of them worked well enough. Then, along came the air fryer and everything changed.

I'm not exaggerating when I say the advent of air frying has literally changed my life. This new technology, introduced by Philips in 2010, uses a patented rapid air circulation innovation that delivers intense, high, allover heat to the entire surface of food. The rate of hot air circulation in the air fryer blows away speeds previously achieved with convection ovens. Philips effectively invented a mechanism by which air conducts heat as efficiently as oil...*without the oil*. The result has been nothing less than a revolution in cooking. This represents a change in the way we think of food that can rightfully be deemed healthy. This book is my own personal celebration of that revolution, as it's played out in my kitchen since I first brought home my own Philips AirFryer.

Care for some crispy breaded and seasoned chicken tenders, without a drop of oil? No problem! How about some crunchy fried bacon, cooked in nothing but its own natural goodness? Of course, sometimes a touch of butter or oil is still called for in a recipe, but for flavor rather than crispiness. My Basil, Tomato and Mozzarella Bruschetta recipe for instance, (under the "Appetizers" section) would still crisp perfectly in the air fryer without the touch of extra virgin olive oil called for in the recipe, but it would lack the rich savory essence of the olive.

The air fryer is the best thing to ever happen to my kitchen and to the nutrition of my friends, family, and dinner party guests. If you've recently joined me in the happy air fryer owner's club, consider the following recipes my welcome gift to our elite bunch. Air frying is the culinary way of the future and it's right here, right now. How great is that?

Using This Book:

The following recipes are arranged roughly by meal categories and food type, which should allow cooks to quickly find the sort of dish they're looking for. In each recipe, you'll find full preparation and cooking instructions, and serving notes. These recipes need not be read in any order, so go ahead and jump around as your mood suits.

As noted in each of the recipes, cooks should be sure to use protective equipment such as tongs, spatulas, and oven mitts where appropriate in handling the hot air fryer and the dishes coming in or out of it. In all cases, make sure to fully read the safety instructions and user manuals that come with any kitchen appliance, to ensure correct usage, safety specifications, and so forth.

Always place foods and baking dishes in the basket of the air fryer, as directed in each of these recipes. Do *not* place cooking food or dishes directly on the air fryer surface, since that would prevent the air from circulating fully around the food. Also, always ensure that any baking dishes or tins used inside the air fryer are oven safe, and that they leave enough room inside the air fryer to allow for full airflow.

In some cases, recipes in this book will call for additional preparation using other cooking methods, such as stovetop sautéing or boiling. However, cooks should never attempt to substitute any cooking method for air frying in these recipes; where the instructions call for air frying, do *not* use an alternative cooking method, because the timing, temperature and measurements will be off. The recipes in this book have all been developed and tested specifically for air frying, and the results would be unpredictable at best with other cooking methods.

All the recipes in this book give temperature directions for Fahrenheit appliances, so if you've got a Celsius appliance, make certain to convert appropriately while following the instructions.

Choosing an Air fryer: The Philips HD9220/26 vs. Everything Else

Philips is the first, the best, and in my opinion, the *only* true air fryer on the market. The innovative oil free air frying method simply did not exist until Philips introduced its patented rapid air technology, so it's little surprise that Philips would still be leading the pack by far. Since Philips released the original HD9220/26 air fryer in 2010, several other brands and manufacturers have jumped into the market with devices claiming to imitate the method. But none of these copycat products, in my opinion, come close to matching the quality, durability, effectiveness and ease of use that comes with the Philips model.

Don't just take my word for it, though. Most other cooks agree with me, if the sales numbers are anything to go by. Even the famously cantankerous, Michelin starred chef, Gordon Ramsey swears by the HD9220/26. With roughly 5 million sold around the world, the original Philips is still the bestselling air fryer on the market, and for good reason. The technology is elegant, one of a kind, and highly efficient thanks to Philips's proprietary "starfish design," which optimizes heat conduction for ideal cooking results. The outcome is perfectly cooked food every time, that's crispy on the outside and succulent on the inside.

Even better for the techno timid among us, the HD9220/26's user interface couldn't be simpler. Clearly marked dials allow chefs to set their specific cooking time and temperature, up to 30 minutes and 390 degrees F, respectively – and then walk away. The air fryer's automatic shut off not only helps ensure safety in the kitchen; it also means that food will never be accidentally burned or overcooked. The device is also completely dishwasher friendly, and its sleek plastic outer shell is easily wiped off by hand.

The versatility of the Philips model also can't be beat. Depending on the dish and the settings, cooks can not only air fry their recipes, but also air grill, air roast, or air bake. The roomy 1.8pound capacity of its basket is more than generous, which is perfect for preparing meals for family or small groups. And of course, being the company that it is, Philips is always quick to help out with excellent customer service if I ever do have a question about usage.

As I said, there are several other devices on the market claiming to achieve "air frying," but I can't in good conscience recommend them. Every recipe in this book has been developed and tested on my trusty Philips HD9220/26, and for my money there is no better value. Philips has consistently lived up to its reputation as a brand that home cooks can trust, and its air fryer is a classic example of why. My whole family loves the Philips and all the tantalizing meals that come out of it, and I know yours will too.

1

BREAKFAST AND BRUNCH

THE CLASSIC BREAKFAST (AIR) FRY UP

Nothing says "good morning" like a heaping plate of fried eggs, crispy bacon and crunchy hash browns. That classic morning combination has fallen out of favor in recent years, partly because few home cooks have time in the morning to use and clean three separate frying pans, and partly because everyone's terrified of the large amounts of oil and grease required to get the fry up just right. The air fryer lets you do all the cooking in one dish, with no messy cleanup, and drastically reduces the oil involved, meaning this downhome favorite can once again become a breakfast time regular. *(Recipe serves 2 people.)*

INGREDIENTS:

6 strips of bacon

1 large potato, peeled, boiled and cubed

1 tablespoon of melted butter

½ tablespoon of flour

Pinch of salt and pepper

2 medium sized eggs

INSTRUCTIONS:

1. Crack the eggs into a ceramic dish or bowl (heat safe and small enough to fit inside the air fryer basket). Set aside.

2. In a separate bowl, combine the potato cubes, melted butter, flour, salt and pepper. Stir until the ingredients are evenly mixed, though not so much that the potatoes become mashed. Set aside.

3.   Line the inside of your air fryer basket with tin foil, leaving at least a ½inch space around the edge of the basket for air to circulate.

4.   Place the strips of bacon flat inside the lined air fryer basket, side by side but not overlapping (they should take up less than half the surface area of the fryer basket, leaving room for other ingredients later on to cook simultaneously).

5.   Set the air fryer to 360 degrees for 10 minutes.

6.   The oil naturally present in the bacon will begin to bubble long before the meat is ready – don't worry. After 10 minutes, the air fryer will shut off. Remove the air frying basket and, using tongs, flip the bacon over to the other side.

7.   While the air frying basket is out, also add the potato mixture – it should fit neatly onto the section of the basket not covered by the bacon.

8.   Set the air fryer to 320 degrees for 15 minutes.

9.   After 15 minutes, remove the frying basket once again; the bacon should now be perfectly crisp and brown. Using tongs, remove the bacon and set aside to cool before serving.

10.   Using tongs or a fork, gently stir the potatoes, which should already be starting to crisp and brown.

11.   In the empty space on the air frying basket left by the bacon, place the ceramic dish (or dishes) containing the eggs.

12.   Set the air fryer back to 320 degrees, for 15 minutes.

13.   When the fryer shuts off, remove the frying basket. The eggs should be perfectly cooked, with firm whites and runny yolks, and the potatoes should be crunchy and golden – the perfect hash browns. The set aside bacon should still be warm, though not too hot to eat.

14.   Serve all together, with additional salt and pepper to taste. And have a terrific morning!

NOTES:

The timing on the bacon can be adjusted – just add a few more minutes if you like your bacon super crispy, or shave a few off if you prefer it more tender. Just remember to use separate dishes for the eggs, and everything will taste delicious. The great breakfast fry up has never tasted so nice, and with so little grease, you can feel good about having it whenever you want!

APPLE CINNAMON EMPANADAS

This south of the border recipe will warm up even the coldest mornings, and give a sweet and energetic start to your day. While these tasty treats are sweet enough to serve for dessert, I've included them in the breakfast section because they're also packed with nutrients and are traditionally enjoyed in the mornings in Mexico. Whenever you choose to whip 'em up, these fruit filled pastries will be big hit every time. *(Recipe serves 2-4 people.)*

INGREDIENTS:

2-3 baking apples, peeled and cubed

1/4 cup of white sugar

2 teaspoons of cinnamon

1 tablespoon of brown sugar

½ tablespoon of cornstarch

1 tablespoon of water

¼ teaspoon of vanilla extract

2 tablespoons of butter or margarine

4 premade empanada dough shells (preparation is chef's choice; Goya or Fargo both work well).

INSTRUCTIONS:

1. Combine white and brown sugar, cinnamon, and cornstarch in a bowl; set aside.

2. Place the peeled and chopped apple cubes in a pot on the stovetop.

3. Cover the apples with the combined dry ingredients, then add vanilla extract, water, and butter; stir thoroughly.

4. Cover the pot and set stove to high heat, until the contents begin to bubble. Once bubbling, decrease heat to low and let simmer until the apples are soft.

5. Remove the pot from the heat and allow to cool until lukewarm.

6. Lay empanada shells flat on a clean counter.

7. Spoon the apple mixture into each of the shells – a good dollop on each, though not so much that the mixture spills over the edges.

8. Fold the empanada shells over so that the apple mixture is fully covered. Seal edges with water and press down with a fork to secure.

9. Cover the basket of the air fryer with a lining of tin foil, leaving at least ½ inch space uncovered around the edges to allow air to circulate. Ideally you want the foil to just be underneath the food, allowing plenty of air circulation.

10. Place the empanadas on the foil in the air fryer basket and set at 350 degrees for 15 minutes.

11. Halfway through, slide the frying basket out and flip the empanadas using a spatula.

12. Remove when golden, and serve directly from the basket onto plates. Eat up while they're hot, and enjoy!

NOTES:

Cooks will argue till the cows come home over which type of baking apple is best for this or that recipe. For these empanadas, I personally enjoy Granny Smith or Jonagold apples when I can find them, though honestly any apple with a good balance of sweetness and tartness will work just fine. These empanadas are hard to mess up, so don't be afraid to experiment!

LIGHT AS AIR BLUEBERRY MUFFINS

Who can resist a good blueberry muffin? Moist and fluffy on the inside, brown and crunchy on the outside, and filled with the goodness of ripe nutritious blueberries, there is simply no better accompaniment to that morning cup of coffee. This air fryer adapted recipe delivers all that, with a fraction of the oil used in most muffin recipes. They're so good, it's difficult to stop at just one – and thankfully, you don't have to. (Recipe serves 1-2 people.)

INGREDIENTS:

½ cup of white sugar

1 ½ cups of all-purpose flour, plus 1 tablespoon

2 teaspoons of baking powder

½ teaspoon of salt

1/3 cup of vegetable oil

1 medium sized egg

¼ cup of unsweetened yogurt

2 teaspoons of vanilla extract

1 cup of fresh, ripe blueberries, rinsed

1 tablespoon of brown sugar

INSTRUCTIONS:

1. Coat the blueberries lightly with 1 tablespoon of flour, shake, and set aside.

2. In a large bowl, mix the white sugar, 1 1/2 cups of flour, baking powder and salt. Stir well to ensure all the dry ingredients are combined evenly.

3. In a separate, smaller bowl, pour oil, then add egg, yogurt, and vanilla extract. Whisk or beat thoroughly, until ingredients are uniformly combined and slightly fluffy.

4. Pour the wet mixture into the larger bowl with the dry ingredients, and combine evenly with a fork or handheld whisk. (Do *not* use an electric beater – you do not want to overmix the batter, or the muffins will come out chewy and dense!)

5. Add the blueberries, and gently fold in with a spatula or wooden spoon.

6. Place silicone baking cups in the air fryer basket. The basket should fit four or five muffin cups comfortably – better to do two batches than to overcrowd!

7. Spoon batter into each of the muffin cups, filling them up about ¾ of the way. Sprinkle a pinch of brown sugar onto the surface of each, for an extra sweet crunch.

8. Set the air fryer to 350 degrees for 10 minutes.

9. After 10 minutes, the air fryer will shut off; remove the basket and test muffins by sticking a toothpick inside – if the toothpick comes out dry, your muffins are ready! If not, reset the air fryer to 320 degrees for 2 minutes, or until the toothpick comes out dry.

10. Remove your finished muffins from the frying basket and set aside to cool; place more muffin tins on the baking tray, and repeat until all your batter is used up (this recipe should make 11 or 1-2 muffins). Serve hot or cold.

NOTES:

These muffins are such a tasty way to start the day. Who knew that blueberries were the best way to chase off the morning blues? They're perfect for those days when you need to take your breakfast on the go, and kids will love them with a glass of milk. They're such a treat, children might even forget that they're eating extremely healthy fruit!

Crunchy Brunchy Breakfast Casserole

This dish is a special one in my family. It's the one I pull out for those rare occasions when everyone is gathered together around the breakfast table with enough time to really savor a hot, delectable dish. The sausage, cheese and breadcrumbs in this casserole compliment the egg perfectly, and I love how the cheesy crust comes out crispy and perfect every time. It's so mouthwateringly good, your family may just want to stay at the breakfast table all day! *(Recipe serves 3-4 people.)*

INGREDIENTS:

6 ounces of raw sweet sausage, squeezed out of the casings

½ cup of bread crumbs (Panko, or any other brand or homemade recipe)

4 eggs

Pinch of salt and pepper

1 cup of shredded cheddar cheese

INSTRUCTIONS:

1. Preheat the air fryer to 350 degrees.

2. In a stovetop pan, cook the raw sausage on medium to high heat for approximately 10 minutes, or until fully cooked, making sure to break up the meat with a wooden spoon while it cooks to prevent clumping. Once cooked, remove from heat and set aside.

3. In a mixing bowl, beat the eggs until fluffy and until the whites and yolks are combined.

4. Stir in the cooked sausage meat, half the cheese, half the bread crumbs, the salt and pepper, making sure that the cheese doesn't clump together and all the ingredients are evenly spread.

5. Pour the mixture into a 6-inch baking dish, then sprinkle the rest of the bread crumbs and shredded cheese on top.

6. Set the baking dish in the air fryer basket – careful not to burn your fingers! – and set the air fryer timer for 20 minutes.

7. After 20 minutes, when the air fryer shuts off, remove the baking dish using oven mitts. The dish will be perfectly cooked, with a golden brown crunchy cheesy top. Serve and enjoy!

NOTES:

This is the ultimate hot breakfast or brunch that will fill your family up for the rest of the day and give a real special occasion feel to the meal. It's a complete meal on its own, and pairs great with a glass of fresh fruit juice – or even a mimosa, if the adults in your group are really feeling indulgent.

Air Fried French Toast Sticks

This recipe is another family favorite. My kids just love crispy, fun, finger foody French toast sticks, and of course the adults in my household (ahem) find them very difficult to resist as well. This meal couldn't be easier or simpler to prepare, even on busy mornings, and with minimal grease required to make them in the air fryer, there's nothing sinful about them! Whether you're cooking for a kitchen full of children, or just for your own French toast loving inner child, this recipe gives a delicious start to the day. *(Recipe serves 3-4 people.)*

INGREDIENTS:

Two slices of white bread, lightly buttered on both sides

2 medium sized eggs

1 pinch of salt

1 teaspoon of cinnamon

½ teaspoon of nutmeg

INSTRUCTIONS:

1. Preheat the air fryer to 350 degrees.
2. Whisk the eggs lightly in a bowl, adding in the salt, cinnamon and nutmeg as you go.
3. Cut your buttered bread into slices. This may be easier to do with scissors than with a knife, and will keep more butter on the bread rather than stuck on a cutting board!

4. One by one, drench each bread strip in the wet mixture, coat and soak thoroughly on all sides. Then, using tongs, arrange them side by side on the air frying basket. They should all fit evenly, closely spaced but not touching. And remember, the air fryer will be extremely hot by now, so don't try to lay the strips down using your bare fingers.

5. Set the timer to 3 minutes.

6. After the 3 minutes are up, the air fryer will shut off. Remove the frying basket and, using a spatula, flip the French toast sticks over.

7. Reset the air fryer to 350 degrees for another 3 minutes.

8. When done, the French toast sticks should be crispy and golden. Serve on plates, with or without maple syrup.

NOTES:

These goodies go perfectly with a little jam, honey, or agave syrup, for those looking for an alternative to maple syrup. They're best when hot, though fine to eat cold as well. Funny enough, there never seem to be any leftovers with these, as they seem to get gobbled up very quickly. You may find yourself hankering to whip up another batch soon. Thank heavens, it couldn't be easier.

STEAK AND EGGS AND CARAMELIZED ONIONS

This breakfast is not for light eaters – then again, everybody's a "hungry man" with this delicious combination of fried eggs, savory browned steak and crispy caramelized onions. Protein packed and filled with nutrients, this is the kind of breakfast that will keep you fueled all day long. And thanks to the air fryer, you can whip up this meal without having to use multiple pans, and with none of the added oil or grease normally required. It doesn't get better than that! *(Recipe serves 2 people.)*

INGREDIENTS:

1 large flank steak (approximately 56 ounces)

1 tablespoon of dry mustard powder

2 medium sized eggs

1 large white onion, washed and sliced thinly (not diced)

Pinch of salt and pepper

INSTRUCTIONS:

1. Rub the flank steak with the dry mustard powder.

2. Place the steak in the air frying basket, as well as the sliced onion. It's fine if the ingredients overlap – the oil from the steak and the moisture from the onions cook perfectly together, each enhancing the flavor of the other.

3. Set the air fryer at 360 degrees for 3 minutes.

4. After 3 minutes, when the fryer shuts off, remove the basket and flip the steak over. Gently stir the onions, which should be starting to brown.

5. Reset the air fryer at 360 degrees for another 3 minutes

6. After 3 minutes, when the fryer shuts off, remove the basket and skewer the steak with a fork. Using scissors, cut the steak into small bite sized chunks, and let them drop back into the air frying basket with the onions.

7. With a spoon or fork, push the steak and onions over to one side of the air frying basket, creating space for one or more heat safe ceramic baking dishes.

8. Crack the eggs into the ceramic dish (or dishes).

9. Set the air fryer at 320 degrees for 15 minutes.

10. After 15 minutes, when the fryer shuts off, the eggs should be perfect – solid whites and runny yolks. The onions will be browned to a delicious caramelized crisp, thanks to the naturally occurring oils from that savory browned steak. Serve directly from the basket, with salt and pepper to taste.

NOTES:

This mouthwatering meal is hearty and filling, a perfect breakfast for those cold winter months when your body needs all the energy it can get. Feel free to adjust the timing according to desired onion crispiness – I prefer just a hint of caramelization on my onions, though others might want them downright blackened. Regardless, rest assured that your steak and eggs will come out wonderfully every time, leaving you filled up and ready for the day!

THE WORLD'S GREATEST MUFFINS

Ok, with apologies to the absolutely awesome blueberry muffins listed elsewhere in this book, it's official: these *are* the world's greatest muffins. The combination of heart healthy oat bran with fresh, nutrient filled blackberries just can't be beat. Rich in fiber, and even richer in flavor, these muffins are a breakfast homerun, and will provide sustained energy throughout the day. Nutritious breakfasts never tasted so sweet!

INGREDIENTS:

2/3 cups of oat bran

1 ½ cups of all-purpose flour

½ teaspoon of baking soda

2 teaspoons of baking powder

½ teaspoon of ground cinnamon

¼ teaspoon of salt

6 tablespoons of unsalted, softened butter

½ cup of white sugar

1 tablespoon of brown sugar

2 large eggs

2 teaspoons of vanilla extract

1 cup of buttermilk

1 ½ cups of blackberries, rinsed and coarsely chopped

INSTRUCTIONS:

1. In a large bowl, combine butter and white sugar with a whisk or electric beater, until fluffy and light.

2. Add vanilla and the eggs, beating until thoroughly combined.

3. In a separate bowl, mix the flour, baking soda, baking powder, cinnamon and salt until all dry ingredients are well incorporated.

4. At a low setting with a hand mixer, or gently whisking, add half of the flour mixture to the eggs. Stir gently, add the buttermilk and then add the remaining flour. Continue to mix until all the ingredients are thoroughly combined, but be careful not to overmix (lest the muffins turn out chewy).

5. Gently fold in the chopped blackberries with a large wooden spoon or spatula.

6. Place sturdy baking cups in the air fryer basket. The basket should fit four or five muffin cups comfortably – better to do two batches than to overcrowd!

7. Spoon batter into each of the muffin cups, filling them up about ¾ of the way. Sprinkle a pinch of brown sugar onto the surface of each, for an extra sweet crunch.

8. Set the air fryer to 350 degrees for 10 minutes.

9. After 10 minutes, the air fryer will shut off; remove the basket and test muffins by sticking a toothpick inside – if the toothpick comes out dry, your muffins are ready! If not, reset the air fryer to 320 degrees for 2 minutes, or until the toothpick comes out dry.

10. Remove your finished muffins from the frying basket and set aside to cool; place more muffin tins on the baking tray, and re-peat until all your batter is used up (this recipe should make 11 or 1-2 muffins). Serve hot or cold.

NOTES:

This is such a nutritious and delicious breakfast, you'll find that one batch goes quickly. If you do have any leftover, these muffins are terrific sliced in half, reheated in your air fryer, and enjoyed with a small pat of margarine or butter. The muffins pack a fantastically healthful punch in a small, compact package, which means they'll leave you with energy for the whole day. They sure beat the cereal based oat bran delivery system! Eat up and have a great morning.

THE ULTIMATE BREAKFAST SANDWICH

Everyone loves a good breakfast sandwich – the classic ham, egg and cheese favorite is a tasty and protein rich way to start off the day, and it can be eaten on the go, which makes it the perfect choice for busy mornings. This air fryer recipe takes the old standard to the next level, with minimal oil and grease, and easy preparation without the use of multiple pans. With one of these breakfast sandwiches, anyone can be a morning person! (Recipe serves 1 person.)

INGREDIENTS:

1 English muffin, sliced in half

1 medium sized egg

1 slice of ham

1 slice of cheddar, American, or provolone cheese

Pinch of salt and pepper

INSTRUCTIONS:

1. Place the English muffins, crusty side up, on the air frying basket side by side.

2. Lay the slice of ham flat on the air frying basket, next to the slices of English muffin.

3. Set the air fryer to 350 degrees for 5 minutes.

4. Once the 5 minutes are up, the air fryer will shut off. Using tongs or a spatula, flip the ham and the slices of English muffin, so that the latter are now crusty side down.

5.   Place the slice of cheese on top of one of the English muffins.

6.   In a small, heat safe ceramic dish, crack the egg. Place the egg dish in the air frying basket next to the muffins and ham.

7.   Set the air fryer to 320 degrees for 15 minutes.

8.   After 15 minutes, when the fryer shuts off, the egg whites should be firm, with runny yolks; the ham perfectly cooked, and the cheese melted over the crusty toasted English muffins.

9.   Using a spatula, remove the cheese-less English muffin slice first, and place on a plate. Layer on the ham and egg, add salt and pepper to taste, then top with the cheese covered English muffin slice.

NOTES:

This recipe couldn't be simpler, and it's fast and easy to whip up multiple batches for the whole family. Wrapped in tin foil, these sandwiches will stay warm and the egg yolks runny for up to two hours, perfect for breakfast on the go.

SUPERFOOD SUPER OMELET

Omelets are just about the most versatile breakfast dish out there, and depending on the fillings, one of the healthiest, as well. Trouble is, they're often difficult to cook smoothly in a regular frying pan. This air fried version could not be easier, since the eggs are able to cook quickly and evenly for a perfect, fluffy consistency. The veggie rich fillings make this a tasty and nutrient packed start to the day, perfect for a high-energy breakfast that won't weigh you down. *(Recipe serves 3-4 people.)*

INGREDIENTS:

6 medium sized eggs
½ cup of grated cheddar cheese
¼ cup of cooked spinach (fresh or frozen; chef's choice)
¼ cup of finely chopped broccoli, lightly steamed
Pinch of salt and pepper

INSTRUCTIONS:

1. Crack the eggs into a large bowl, and beat until fluffy and until whites and yolks are evenly combined.

2. Add the spinach, broccoli, and cheese. Stir until mixed.

3. Pour the mixture into a 6-inch nonstick baking pan that has been sprayed lightly with cooking spray. (The pan should be large enough to fit all the ingredients with an inch or more to spare, but small enough to fit inside the air fryer basket.)

4. Place the pan inside the air fryer basket.

5. Set the air fryer to 360 degrees for 15 minutes.

6.   After 15 minutes, the air fryer will shut off and the omelet should be golden and crisp on top. Using a spatula to help it along, slide the omelet onto a plate. Slice into serving portions, add salt and pepper to taste, and eat while hot!

NOTES:

This breakfast will give a power start to any morning, and it's especially good before long workdays when you know you'll need to be your sharpest self. Don't let the gooey melted cheese or fluffy eggs fool you – this omelet is as healthy as it gets, a breakfast fit for a champion!

GREEN EGGS AND HAM OMELET

Don't worry, the eggs aren't really green – or at least, they shouldn't be! But the addition of verdant scallions in this recipe adds a wonderful tang, not to mention a healthy dose of chlorophyll, bringing the classic ham and cheese omelet to the next level. A balanced and savory breakfast, this recipe couldn't be simpler – or more delicious. *(Recipe serves 3-4 people.)*

INGREDIENTS:

6 medium sized eggs

½ cup of grated cheddar cheese

1/3 cup of cured ham, sliced and cubed into small pieces

¼ cup of finely chopped scallions

Pinch of salt and pepper

INSTRUCTIONS:

1. Crack the eggs into a large bowl, and beat until fluffy and until whites and yolks are evenly combined.

2. Add the ham, cheese, and scallions. Stir until mixed.

3. Pour the mixture into a 6-inch nonstick baking pan sprayed very lightly with cooking spray. (The pan should be large enough to fit all the ingredients with an inch or more to spare, but small enough to fit inside the air fryer basket.)

4. Place the pan inside the air fryer basket.

5. Set the air fryer to 360 degrees for 15 minutes.

6. After 15 minutes, the air fryer will shut off and the omelet should be golden and crisp on top. Using a spatula to help it along, slide the omelet onto a plate. Slice into serving portions, add salt and pepper to taste, and eat up while hot!

NOTES:

Feel free to play with the ratios in this one – a little less scallions, a little extra ham or cheese – depending on personal preference. This recipe is almost impossible to get wrong, so don't be afraid to experiment. However you take your air fried "green eggs and ham" omelet, rest easy knowing you've made a breakfast that's every bit as nutritious as it is delicious!

MEAT LOVER'S BREAKFAST DELIGHT

This is another omelet, and a family favorite at my house. It's protein packed and nutritious as it goes, though with the high content of meat it's probably best to save this one for weekends, or at least days when you can follow up your breakfast with enough time to rest and digest. All that said, it's my family's favorite for a reason – meaty and cheesy and oh so delicious, this is a breakfast to satisfy even the most insatiable carnivores! *(Recipe serves 3-4 people.)*

INGREDIENTS:

6 medium sized eggs

½ cup of grated cheddar cheese

3 precooked breakfast sausages, sliced into bite sized pieces

8 strips of bacon, sliced into bite sized pieces

Pinch of salt and pepper

INSTRUCTIONS:

1. Crack the eggs into a large bowl, and beat until fluffy and until whites and yolks are evenly combined.

2. Add the sausage, bacon, and cheese. Stir until mixed, and make sure the bacon pieces are separated and not stuck together.

3. Pour the mixture into a nonstick baking pan (large enough to fit all the ingredients with an inch or more to spare, but small enough to fit inside the air fryer basket.)

4. Place the pan inside the air fryer basket.

5.   Set the air fryer to 360 degrees for 15 minutes.

6.   After 15 minutes, the air fryer will shut off and the omelet should be golden and crisp on top. Using a spatula to help it along, slide the omelet to a plate. Slice into serving portions, add salt and pepper to taste, and eat up while hot!

NOTES:

This omelet goes great with a side of fresh fruit or a glass of juice, to balance out the wonderful saltiness in the meats. The protein rich breakfast will power you through the whole day – though be sure to take a few minutes after eating to digest; this is probably not the best breakfast to eat right before a workout. But if you like meat, there is simply no better omelet to quench your cravings. Enjoy!

BREAKFAST SANDWICH FIT FOR A QUEEN

This is the kind of breakfast I imagine royalty enjoying every morning. And for me at least, the luxurious combination of ripe avocado, smoked salmon and fluffy scrambled eggs is good enough to make me *feel* like royalty. So go on, pamper yourself and enjoy this breakfast delight. You'll feel healthy, wealthy and wise in every way. *(Recipe serves 1 person.)*

INGREDIENTS:

1 English muffin, sliced in half

1 medium sized egg

½ ripe avocado, sliced and lightly mashed

1 thick slice of smoked salmon

Pinch of salt and pepper

INSTRUCTIONS:

1. Place the English muffins, crusty side up, on the air frying basket side by side.

2. In a small, heat safe ceramic dish, crack the egg and beat or whisk until fluffy, and until white and yolk are evenly combined.

3. Set the air fryer to 360 degrees for 10 minutes.

4. Once the 10 minutes are up, the air fryer will shut off. Using a fork, gently scramble the half cooked egg in the baking dish. With a spatula, flip the slices of English muffin, so that they are now crusty side down.

5. Set the air fryer to 320 degrees for 10 minutes.

6.   After 10 minutes, when the fryer shuts off, the scrambled eggs should be firmly cooked, but still fluffy; and the English muffins perfectly toasted.

7.   Using a spatula, place one of the English muffin slices on a serving plate; then spread the sliced and mashed avocado on top.

8.   Scoop the scrambled eggs out of the baking tin and onto the avocado, then layer the smoked salmon on top of the eggs. Add salt and pepper to taste.

9.   Top with the second slice of toasted English muffin, close sandwich, and enjoy while the eggs are still hot!

NOTES:

In a perfect world, I could enjoy this breakfast every morning. But since neither avocados nor smoked salmon are cheap, it's probably best to save this recipe for special occasions. Whenever you have them, these sandwiches are easy, simple and fast to prepare, so it's no trouble to make extra batches when you're cooking for friends or family. Long live this queenly breakfast!

AIR FRIED BANANA AND FRENCH TOAST SANDWICH

Here's another recipe that's wonderful for special occasions, and will always be a big hit with kids around. The combination of cinnamon spiced French toast with caramelized bananas and a dollop of whipped cream is just too good to resist – and it packs a nutritious punch as well. A wholesome and balanced breakfast has never tasted so sweet! *(Recipe serves 1 person.)*

INGREDIENTS:

Two slices of white bread

2 medium sized eggs

1 teaspoon of cinnamon

½ a ripe banana, peeled and sliced into bite sized chunks

1 tablespoon of brown sugar

¼ cup of whipped cream

INSTRUCTIONS:

1. Preheat the air fryer to 350 degrees.

2. In a small bowl, tumble the banana chunks with the brown sugar, stirring and shaking until the banana is fully covered with a dusting of sugar; set aside.

3. Crack the eggs into a separate, large mixing bowl, whisk until fluffy and until the whites and yolks are thoroughly combined.

4. Add in the cinnamon, and continue stirring until completely blended.

5.   One by one, soak the bread slices in the egg mixture, coating and soaking thoroughly on both sides, then place on the air fryer basket, making sure not to touch the hot surface with your fingers.

6.   The two egg soaked bread slices should cover half of the air frying basket; on the other half, lay the sugarcoated banana chunks, and set the air fryer timer for 10 minutes.

7.   After 10 minutes, when the air fryer shuts off, the bread slices should be browning nicely, and the bananas beginning to caramelize; using a spatula, flip both the bread slices and all the banana chunks.

8.   Reset the air fryer at 350 degrees for another 10 minutes.

9.   When finished, the banana chunks should be crispy on the outside, and warm and gooey on the inside; and the French toast slices should be a beautiful golden brown on all sides.

10.   Using a spatula, place one of the browned French toast slices onto a serving plate, then spoon the whipped cream on top and spread evenly.

11.   Scoop the caramelized banana chunks onto the whipped cream, and cover with the second French toast slice. Enjoy while it's hot, with a knife and fork, or your bare hands if it's cool enough to handle and you're okay getting a little messy.

NOTES:

This recipe is basically the definition of "yummy." Kids will love it, and it's a great treat to pull out for a child's birthday breakfast – candles will even fit easily into the top! No need to tell them that that this is a potassium rich and healthy way to satisfy a sweet tooth. As for adults, I don't care how old you are – this scrumptious delight will be sure to bring out the kid in you, so eat up and enjoy!

SUMMER VEGETABLE CHEESY TART

Don't mind the name. This savory, creamy cheesy dish is plenty filling enough to enjoy in the winter months, though it's also light enough for the warmer seasons. The eggplant, tomato and zucchini keep this tart light and airy, and are perfectly balanced by the creamy filling and cheesy topping. Enjoy – and feel great! *(Recipe serves 3-4 people.)*

INGREDIENTS:

Premade savory crust, chilled and rolled flat to make a 6-inch pie crust (Pillsbury and Marie Callender's both offer great options, or feel free to use any other brand or homemade recipe).

2 eggs

¼ cup of milk

Pinch of salt and pepper

¼ cup of cooked eggplant, finely chopped

¼ cup of cooked zucchini, finely chopped

¼ cup of raw tomato, finely chopped

¼ cup of shredded mozzarella cheese

¼ cup of shredded cheddar cheese

INSTRUCTIONS:

1. Preheat the air fryer to 360 degrees.
2. Press the premade crust into a 6-inch pie tin, or any appropriately sized glass or ceramic heat safe dish. Press and trim at the edges if necessary.

3.   With a fork, pierce several holes in the dough to allow air circulation and prevent cracking of the crust while cooking.

4.   In a mixing bowl, beat the eggs until fluffy and until the yolks and white are evenly combined.

5.   Add milk, eggplant, zucchini, tomato, salt and pepper, and half the cheddar and mozzarella cheese to the eggs.

6.   Set the rest of the cheese aside for now, and stir the mixture until completely blended.

7.   Pour the mixture into the tart crust, slowly and carefully to avoid splashing. The mixture should almost fill the crust, but not completely – leaving a ¼ inch of crust at the edges.

8.   Place the pie dish into the basket of the sir fryer. Set the timer for 15 minutes.

9.   After 15 minutes, the air fryer will shut off, and the tart will already be firm and the crust beginning to brown. Sprinkle the rest of the cheddar and mozzarella cheese on top of the tart filling.

10. Reset the air fryer at 360 degrees for 5 minutes.

11. After 5 minutes, when the air fryer shuts off, the cheese will have formed an exquisite crust on top and the tart will be golden brown and perfect. Remove from the air fryer using oven mitts or tongs, and set on a heat safe surface to cool.

NOTES:

This dish is so simple, but so elegant. The flavors blend perfectly and the consistency comes out excellent every time in the air fryer. It's also packed with vitamins, minerals and nutrients. It's hard to tell in all that creamy cheesy goodness, but true! Savor this lunch, it's worth it.

TOMATO SALMON QUICHE

The wholesome goodness of fresh tomatoes and nutrient packed salmon meet all the decadence of creamy, cheesy, crispy topped quiche in this delightful recipe. This is the perfect lunch for when you really want to treat your body right – and to treat your taste buds even better! *(Recipe serves 3-4 people.)*

INGREDIENTS:

Premade quiche crust, chilled and rolled flat to make a 6-inch pie crust (Pillsbury and Marie Callender's both offer great options, or feel free to use any other brand or homemade recipe).

2 eggs

¼ cup of milk

Pinch of salt and pepper

5 ounces of cooked salmon, either canned or fresh and lightly grilled

1 large tomato, washed and diced

¼ cup of shredded mozzarella cheese

¼ cup of shredded American cheese

INSTRUCTIONS:

1. Preheat the air fryer to 360 degrees.

2. Press the premade crust into a 6-inch pie tin, or any appropriately sized glass or ceramic heat safe dish. Press and trim at the edges if necessary.

3. With a fork, pierce several holes in the dough to allow air circulation and prevent cracking of the crust while cooking.

4. In a mixing bowl, beat the eggs until fluffy and until the yolks and white are evenly combined.

5. Add milk, tomatoes, salt, pepper, salmon, and half the American and mozzarella cheese to the eggs. As you stir, flake and break the salmon up into bite sized chunks.

6. Set the rest of the cheese aside for now, and stir the mixture until completely blended. Make sure the salmon is not clumped together, but rather spread among the other ingredients.

7. Pour the mixture into the pie crust, slowly and carefully to avoid splashing. The mixture should almost fill the crust, but not completely – leaving a ¼ inch of crust at the edges.

8. Set the air fryer timer for 15 minutes.

9. After 15 minutes, the air fryer will shut off, and the quiche will already be firm and the crust beginning to brown. Sprinkle the rest of the American and mozzarella cheese on top of the quiche filling.

10. Reset the air fryer at 360 degrees for 5 minutes.

11. After 5 minutes, when the air fryer shuts off, the cheese will have formed an exquisite crust on top and the quiche will be golden brown and perfect. Remove from the air fryer using oven mitts or tongs, and set on a heat safe surface to cool for a few minutes before cutting.

NOTES:

This is a wonderful lunch any time of year – light enough for summer, but plenty warm and filling for wintertime. Your friends, family, guests or coworkers will have a hard time believing you whipped up this delicacy so easily – but they sure won't complain when you offer them a slice!

2

APPETIZERS AND SMALL BITES

BASIL, TOMATO AND MOZZARELLA BRUSCHETTA

These delectable bites are light enough for a predinner appetizer, though they also do great on their own as a featured snack. I love the combination of juicy fresh tomatoes with crusty bread and aromatic basil, and the creamy mozzarella adds a truly luxurious texture to this dish. Best of all, it couldn't be easier to prepare, and they're as healthy as they are delicious! *(Recipe serves 3-4 people.)*

INGREDIENTS:

3 medium sized ripe red tomatoes, rinsed and diced

½ loaf of French bread or baguette

1 clove of fresh garlic, peeled and finely minced

3 ounces of fresh mozzarella cheese, sliced thick

1 tablespoon of extra virgin olive oil

10 fresh basil leaves, rinsed, patted dry and finely chopped

½ teaspoon of dry oregano

Pinch of salt

INSTRUCTIONS:

1.   Cover the basket of the air fryer with a lining of tin foil, leaving the edges uncovered to allow air to circulate through the basket.

2.   Preheat the air fryer to 370 degrees.

3.   In a mixing bowl, combine the diced tomatoes, olive oil, salt, oregano, garlic, and basil. Stir thoroughly and set aside.

4. Cut the French bread into slices approximately 1inch thick – there should be 6-8 slices, depending on the bread.

5. Spoon some of the tomato mixture onto each slice of bread, drizzling all over the surface, then top each one with one of the mozzarella slices.

6. Place the covered bread slices on the foil lined air fryer basket, evenly spaced – it's fine if the crusts are touching; they won't stick together thanks to the olive oil.

7. Set the air fryer timer to 5 minutes.

8. After 5 minutes, when the air fryer shuts off, remove the bruschetta with tongs and set on a serving plate. Enjoy while hot!

NOTES:

For the wine lovers out there, these bruschetta go brilliantly with a crisp glass of chardonnay. I love the combined textures of the creamy cheese with the perfectly toasted bread, together with the juicy warm tomatoes. It's so fresh, so simple, and so healthy. There's nothing not to love about this dish!

SPICY BLACK BEAN EMPANADAS

This is a dream come true snack for hungry vegetarians – or for anyone, really, who likes hot spicy black beans perfectly mixed with onions and peppers in a crispy, delicious fried outer shell. In other words, this dish is for everyone! And thanks to the air fryer, it's a terrifically healthy way to pack a ton of protein into a small bite. *(Recipe serves 2-4 people.)*

INGREDIENTS:

½ cup of cooked black beans, drained and rinsed

¼ cup of raw white onions, sliced and finely diced

1 teaspoon of red chili powder

½ teaspoon of paprika

½ teaspoon of garlic salt

4 premade empanada dough shells (preparation is chef's choice; Goya or Fargo both work well).

INSTRUCTIONS:

1.   In a deep stovetop saucepan, sauté the black beans at medium heat. Add in the onions, stirring continuously with a wooden spoon, then add the red chili powder, paprika, and garlic salt.

2.   Remove the saucepan from the stovetop as soon as the beans are hot, the onions are soft, and the spices are releasing their fragrances. Do not overcook – you want the beans to remain moist and juicy! Cover the saucepan and let stand on a heat safe surface for a few minutes.

3.   Lay empanada shells flat on a clean counter.

4. Spoon the spiced cooked beans and onions from the saucepan into the empanada shells– a heaping spoonful on each, though not so much that the mixture spills over the edges.

5. Fold the empanada shells over so that the spiced beans are fully covered. Seal edges with water and press down with a fork to secure.

6. Cover the basket of the air fryer with a lining of tin foil, leaving at least a ½inch edge uncovered to allow air to circulate.

7. Place the empanadas in the foil lined air fryer basket and set at 350 degrees for 15 minutes.

8. Halfway through, slide the frying basket out and flip the empanadas using a spatula.

9. Remove when golden, and serve directly from the basket onto plates.

NOTES:

These awesome empanadas will keep their crunch and flavor just fine once cooled, so don't think twice about wrapping them in some tin foil and taking them with you on the go. Hot or cold, the shells will be crispy and delicious, and the spiced beans will be succulent and juicy. Enjoy anytime, anywhere!

BACON WRAPPED SHRIMP BITES

Fans of the sitcom *Parks and Recreation* will recognize bacon wrapped shrimp as one of Ron Swanson's preferred appetizers – or, as the mustachioed character puts it, "My number one favorite food wrapped around my number three favorite food." That's pretty much exactly the way I feel, and this recipe is all the better because it is so extremely simple to prepare at home. Bring 'em on! *(Recipe serves 3-4 people.)*

INGREDIENTS:

1-2 jumbo shrimp, rinsed and peeled from their shells

1-2 strips of thin sliced bacon

½ medium sized lemon

½ teaspoon of garlic flavored salt

INSTRUCTIONS:

1. Cover the basket of the air fryer with a lining of tin foil, leaving the edges uncovered to allow air to circulate through the basket.

2. Preheat the air fryer to 350 degrees.

3. One by one, starting with the tail end of the shrimp, wrap the bacon around the shrimp, overlapping as you approach the top of the shrimp.

4. Lay each wrapped shrimp, seam side down, on the foil lined surface of the air fryer basket; the dozen should fit snuggly without overlapping, though it's fine if the sides touch a little.

5. Squeeze the lemon juice over all the wrapped shrimp, and sprinkle the garlic salt on top.

6. Set the air fryer timer to 5 minutes.

7. After five minutes, when the air fryer shuts off, turn each of the wrapped shrimp over using tongs.

8. Reset the air fryer to 350 degrees for another 5 minutes.

9. After 5 minutes, when the air fryer shuts off, the wrapped shrimp will be succulent and perfect, and the bacon crisp and juicy around them. Set on a plate using tongs and eat while hot.

NOTES:

Every bite of this delicious treat is better than the last, so don't be surprised if you find yourself hankering for second helpings and thirds! These are a wonderful party snack, but I won't tell anyone if you just want to enjoy a whole batch for yourself.

SALT AND PEPPER CRISPY CALAMARI

Nothing says "appetizer party" like a basket of crunchy on the outside, juicy on the inside, crispy fried squid. This recipe gets the balance just so, with a touch of lemon and Old Bay seasoning in the mix that hits all the right flavor notes. Give your friends, family or guests a treat and whip up a batch today! *(Recipe serves 2-3 people.)*

INGREDIENTS:

1 cup of baby squid, with the tentacles separated from the hoods

½ cup of semolina flour

2 medium sized eggs

Pinch of salt and pepper

½ medium sized lemon

1 teaspoon of Old Bay seasoning

INSTRUCTIONS:

1. Cover the basket of the air fryer with a lining of tin foil, leaving the edges uncovered to allow air to circulate through the basket.

2. Preheat the air fryer to 350 degrees.

3. In a mixing bowl, beat the eggs until fluffy and until the yolks and whites are fully combined. Squeeze in the juice from the lemon, stir thoroughly, and set aside.

4. In a separate mixing bowl, combine the semolina flour, bay seasoning, salt and pepper, and set aside.

5. One by one, dip each piece of squid into the bowl with dry ingredients, coating all sides; then submerge into the bowl with wet

ingredients, then dip again into the dry ingredients. This double coating will ensure an extra crisp and delicious air fry!

6. Lay the coated squid pieces on the foil covering the air fryer basket, in a single flat layer.

7. Set the air fryer timer for 20 minutes.

8. Shake the handle of the air fryer basket several times during cooking, to jostle the calamari and ensure a good even fry.

9. After 20 minutes, the calamari should be crispy, golden brown and perfect. Serve directly from the fryer basket and enjoy while they're hot!

NOTES:

I personally love to chow down on these just as they are, or maybe with a little more lemon juice squeezed over the crispy delicious calamari just before eating. For those who want a more substantial condiment pairing, cocktail sauce is, of course, a classic match and ketchup works great, too. Enjoy this seafood delight, and wow your guests!

CRISPY CHICKEN SPRING ROLLS

These crispy finger foods will liven up any party or predinner cocktail hour, though they're also a great standalone meal all on their own. I love all the crunchy fresh veggies included in this recipe, not to mention how easy they are to prepare and serve. The touch of ginger and a little sugar helps give this savory snack the perfect sweet kick. *(Recipe serves 3-4 people.)*

INGREDIENTS:

1 large breast of chicken, approximately 4 ounces, grilled

1 stalk of celery, rinsed and sliced thin in julienned pieces

1 medium sized carrot, peeled and grated

1 teaspoon of fresh ginger, minced

1 teaspoon of sugar

1 teaspoon of chicken stock powder

1 egg

1 teaspoon of corn starch

6 spring roll wrappers (any brand will do, I like Blue Dragon or Tasty Joy, both available through Target or Walmart, or any large grocery chain)

INSTRUCTIONS:

1. Cover the basket of the air fryer with a lining of tin foil, leaving the edges uncovered to allow air to circulate through the basket.

2. Preheat the air fryer to 360 degrees.

3. Cut the grilled chicken into very small chunks.

4. In a mixing bowl, combine the chicken with the shredded celery and carrot, then add the minced ginger, the sugar, and the chicken stock powder. Combine thoroughly until all ingredients are evenly mixed. Set aside.

5. In a separate bowl, beat the egg until fluffy and until the yolk and white are combined. Add the cornstarch and mix until the ingredients thicken. Set aside.

6. Spoon even amounts of the chicken and vegetable filling into each spring roll wrapper, then roll up and seal the seams with the egg and cornstarch mixture.

7. Place each roll on the foil lined air fryer basket.

8. Set the air fryer timer to 7 minutes. During cooking, shake the handle of the fryer basket several times to ensure a nice even surface crisp.

9. After 7 minutes, when the air fryer shuts off, the spring rolls should be golden brown and perfect. Remove with tongs and serve while hot.

NOTES:

A little sweet chili dipping sauce goes perfectly with these, or some soy sauce for those who prefer a saltier pairing. However you eat these spring rolls, trust me, you won't be able to stop at just one. But they're nice and healthy with no added grease, so have at 'em!

CRUNCHY VEGETARIAN SPRING ROLLS

Herbivores and meat eaters alike can't say no to a bite of hot, crunchy, veggie spring roll goodness. The mushrooms and beans sprouts in these are an awesome flavor combination with the other ingredients, especially with that touch of ginger. *(Recipe serves 3-4 people.)*

INGREDIENTS:

¼ cup of brown or white button mushrooms, rinsed, steamed and finely diced

¼ cup of bean sprouts, rinsed

1 stalk of celery, rinsed and sliced thin in julienned pieces

1 medium sized carrot, peeled and grated

1 teaspoon of fresh ginger, minced

1 teaspoon of sugar

1 teaspoon of vegetable stock powder

1 egg

1 teaspoon of corn starch

6 spring roll wrappers (any brand will do, I like Blue Dragon or Tasty Joy, both available through Target or Walmart, or any large grocery chain)

INSTRUCTIONS:

1. Cover the basket of the air fryer with a lining of tin foil, leaving the edges uncovered to allow air to circulate through the basket.

2. Preheat the air fryer to 360 degrees.

3. In a mixing bowl, combine the mushrooms, beansprouts, shredded celery and carrot, then add the minced ginger, the sugar, and

the vegetable stock powder. Combine thoroughly until all ingredients are evenly mixed. Set aside.

4. In a separate bowl, beat the egg until fluffy and until the yolk and white are combined. Add the cornstarch and mix until the ingredients thicken. Set aside.

5. Spoon even amounts of the vegetable filling into each spring roll wrapper, then roll up and seal the seams with the egg and cornstarch mixture.

6. Place each roll on the foil lined air fryer basket.

7. Set the air fryer timer to 7 minutes. During cooking, shake the handle of the fryer basket several times to ensure a nice even surface crisp.

8. After 7 minutes, when the air fryer shuts off, the spring rolls should be golden brown and perfect. Remove with tongs and serve while hot.

NOTES:

A little sweet chili dipping sauce goes perfectly with these, or some soy sauce for those who prefer a saltier pairing. Any way you serve them, these spring rolls will be hugely popular with your friends, family, or party guests. Enjoy!

PORK WONTON WONDERFUL

These delicious little pork filled wonton bites go wonderfully with the above spring rolls if you want to keep an Asian food theme through your cocktail party or snack fest. The combination of the apples with the pork is so good, and so unexpected, your family, friends or guests will be delighted with your inventive offering. *(Recipe serves 3-4 people.)*

INGREDIENTS:

8 wanton wrappers (Leasa brand works great, though any will do)

4 ounces of minced pork, browned

1 medium sized green apple

1 cup of water, for wetting the wanton wrappers

1 tablespoon of vegetable oil

½ tablespoon of oyster sauce

1 tablespoon of soy sauce

Large pinch of ground white pepper

INSTRUCTIONS:

1. Cover the basket of the air fryer with a lining of tin foil, leaving the edges uncovered to allow air to circulate through the basket.

2. Preheat the air fryer to 350 degrees.

3. In a small mixing bowl, combine the oyster sauce, soy sauce, and white pepper, then add in the minced pork and stir thoroughly. Cover and set in the fridge to marinate for at least 15 minutes.

4. Peel and core the apple, and slice into small cubes – smaller than bite sized chunks.

5. Add the apples to the marinating meat mixture, and combine thoroughly.

6. Spread the wonton wrappers, and fill each with a large spoonful of the filling. Wrap the wontons into triangles, so that the wrappers fully cover the filling, and seal with a small amount of water.

7. Coat each filled and wrapped wonton thoroughly with the vegetable oil, to help ensure a nice crispy fry.

8. Place the wontons on the foil lined air fryer basket.

9. Set the air fryer timer to 25 minutes.

10. Halfway through cooking time, shake the handle of the air fryer basket vigorously to jostle the wontons and ensure even frying.

11. After 25 minutes, when the air fryer shuts off, the wontons will be crispy golden brown on the outside and juicy and delicious on the inside. Serve directly from the air fryer basket and enjoy while hot.

NOTES:

These are wonderful served with a little soy sauce for dipping, or oyster sauce for those who want a little more sweet with their savory. Make sure you serve napkins with these treats, too. Though they're the perfect finger food, they do make crumbs and you won't want to lose any of this crispy goodness to the carpet.

CRAVEWORTHY CRAB CAKES

Ok, time for a confession. I'm pretty much addicted to this recipe for air fried crab cakes. One bite, and I just can't stop – and yes, that does mean that I have, at times, consumed an entire batch of these treats all by myself. For those who think they can control themselves enough to share, these crab cakes make a great appetizer for any party or predinner gathering. *(Recipe serves 3-4 people.)*

INGREDIENTS:

1 cup of lump crab meat

2 stalks of green onions, rinsed and minced

3 cloves of garlic, peeled and finely minced

½ a medium sized lime

2 tablespoons of mayonnaise

2 medium sized eggs

1 teaspoon of fresh grated ginger

½ cup of breadcrumbs (Panko, or any other brand or homemade recipe)

2 teaspoons of oyster sauce

2 teaspoons of spicy mustard

Pinch of ground black pepper

INSTRUCTIONS:

1. Cover the basket of the air fryer with a lining of tin foil, leaving the edges uncovered to allow air to circulate through the basket.

2. Preheat the air fryer to 350 degrees.

3. In a small mixing bowl, beat the eggs until fluffy and until the yolks and whites are thoroughly combined.

4. Place the crab meat in a large mixing bowl, and squeeze the juice from the lime over the crab.

5. Add in the mayonnaise, onions, garlic, ginger, oyster sauce, mustard, and black pepper. Stir thoroughly, until all the ingredients are evenly combined.

6. Form the mixture into patties. The recipe should make between 4 and 8, depending on how large or small you size them.

7. Dunk each of the crab mix patties into the beaten eggs, and then roll in the breadcrumbs, coating thoroughly on all sides.

8. Set the coated crab cakes on the lined surface of the air fryer basket, side by side and not overlapping.

9. Set the air fryer timer to 5 minutes.

10. After 5 minutes, using a spatula, flip the crab cakes over to ensure a nice even fry.

11. Reset the air fryer to 350 degrees for another 5 minutes.

12. After 5 minutes, the crab cakes will be perfect – golden brown and crispy on the outside, and tantalizingly juicy on the inside. Remove from the air fryer basket using a spatula and serve hot or cold.

NOTES:

These are the perfect special occasion accompaniment to a champagne toast, and if you shape the crab cakes large enough they're filling enough to serve as a full meal. I really can't get enough of this delicious recipe, and I know you'll love it, too.

PERFECT (AIR) FRIED PICKLES

Fried pickles have recently become trendy with the hipster set, but this recipe has actually been in my family for generations. My grandmother loved to serve up a platter of fried pickles to her friends over bridge games, and I know they're the kicker that makes my Super Bowl parties a hit. *(Recipe serves 4 people.)*

INGREDIENTS:

2 large kosher dill pickles, sliced into bite sized pieces

1 cup of breadcrumbs (Panko brand works well)

2 medium sized eggs

Pinch of ground white pepper

1 teaspoon of curry powder

INSTRUCTIONS:

1. Cover the basket of the air fryer with a lining of tin foil, leaving the edges uncovered to allow air to circulate through the basket.

2. Preheat the air fryer to 350 degrees.

3. In a mixing bowl, beat the eggs until fluffy and until the yolks and whites are fully combined, and set aside.

4. In a separate mixing bowl, combine the breadcrumbs, curry, and pepper, and set aside.

5. One by one, dip each piece of pickle into the bowl with dry ingredients, coating all sides; then submerge into the bowl with wet ingredients, then dip again into the dry ingredients. This double coating will ensure an extra crisp and delicious air fry!

6. Lay the coated pickle pieces on the foil covering the air fryer basket, in a single flat layer.

7. Set the air fryer timer for 15 minutes.

8. Shake the handle of the air fryer basket several times during cooking, to jostle the pickles and ensure a good even fry.

9. After 15 minutes, the pickles should be crispy, golden brown and perfect. Serve and enjoy while they're hot!

NOTES:

These go great with a little ranch dip, but really the hot battered pickles are juicy enough on the inside not to need any. The crunch when you bite into one of these is absolutely fantastic, but be sure to have a napkin on hand! Eat up and enjoy.

AIR FRIED ONION RINGS

Ah, the classic onion ring! Is there any better accompaniment to a good burger? I think not, which is why I've spent years perfecting this recipe for delicious battered onion rings air fried to a perfect crisp. The touch of garlic and pepper in these give them a wonderful kick, and a terrific twist on the traditional side. *(Recipe serves 4-6 people.)*

INGREDIENTS:

2 large white onions, peeled and sliced, with the rings separated

1 cup of breadcrumbs (Panko brand works well)

2 medium sized eggs

1 teaspoon of ground black pepper

1 teaspoon of garlic powder

INSTRUCTIONS:

1. Cover the basket of the air fryer with a lining of tin foil, leaving the edges uncovered to allow air to circulate through the basket.

2. Preheat the air fryer to 350 degrees.

3. In a mixing bowl, beat the eggs until fluffy and until the yolks and whites are fully combined, and set aside.

4. In a separate mixing bowl, combine the breadcrumbs, garlic powder, and pepper, and set aside.

5. One by one, dip each piece of onion ring into the bowl with dry ingredients, coating all sides; then submerge into the bowl with wet ingredients, then dip again into the dry ingredients. This double coating will ensure an extra crisp and delicious air fry!

6.   Lay the coated onion rings on the foil covering the air fryer basket.

7.   Set the air fryer timer for 15 minutes.

8.   Shake the handle of the air fryer basket several times during cooking, to jostle the onion rings and ensure a good even fry.

9.   After 15 minutes, the onions should be crispy, golden brown and perfect. Serve and enjoy while they're hot!

NOTES:

A little ketchup for dipping, and these onion rings are pure breaded heaven. Nothing beats the sweet, tangy crunch when you bite into one of these – or better yet, stick it straight between your burger and the bun, and put this "side dish" in center stage. Yum!

PIGS IN A BLANKET

A good cocktail wienie wrapped in hot, flaky pastry dough and crisped to perfection is a standard party staple for good reason! These appetizers are as delicious as they are fun to eat, and kids especially love bite sized pastry wrapped hot dogs. This recipe couldn't be easier, so have fun and enjoy! *(Recipe serves 4-6 people.)*

INGREDIENTS:

8 small cocktail weenies or mini hot dogs

8 sheets of flaky pastry dough (Pillsbury Crescent rolls work wonderfully, or any other brand or home recipe will do)

¼ cup of water

1 tablespoon of vegetable oil

INSTRUCTIONS:

1. Cover the basket of the air fryer with a lining of tin foil, leaving the edges uncovered to allow air to circulate through the basket.

2. Preheat the air fryer to 350 degrees.

3. Roll each of the cocktail wienies or mini hot dogs into a sheet of the pastry dough, wrapping them snugly and sealing with a touch of water if needed.

4. Coat each wrapped weenie with an even layer of vegetable oil over the surface of the pastry, to ensure a nice crisp fry.

5. Arrange the wrapped wienies on the foil lined surface of the air fryer, side by side and not touching (you don't want the pastry to stick together as they expand).

6. Set the air fryer timer to 15 minutes.

7. After 15 minutes, the pastry crust should be golden brown and the hotdogs juicy and perfect. Remove from the fryer basket with tongs and serve hot or cold.

NOTES:

A little ketchup or mustard is perfect for dipping, though I actually prefer these without any condiments at all. No party is truly complete without a tray of these yummy pigs in the blanket, so enjoy giving your guests exactly what they want!

CRISPY FLAKY CHEESE ROLLS

This kid friendly appetizer is absolutely scrumptious, a wonderful pairing with the pigs in the blanket, or all by themselves for a cheesy, crispy, finger food snack. Any kind of cheese will work fine for the filling, though I'm partial to the sharp combo of cheddar and Swiss. *(Recipe serves 4-6 people.)*

INGREDIENTS:

¼ cup of grated cheddar cheese

¼ cup of grated Swiss cheese

8 sheets of flaky pastry dough (Pillsbury Crescent rolls work wonderfully, or any other brand or home recipe will do)

¼ cup of water

1 tablespoon of vegetable oil

INSTRUCTIONS:

1. Cover the basket of the air fryer with a lining of tin foil, leaving the edges uncovered to allow air to circulate through the basket.

2. Preheat the air fryer to 350 degrees.

3. In a mixing bowl, combine the shredded cheddar and Swiss cheeses, so that they are evenly distributed.

4. Spoon a helping of the mixed cheeses into each sheet of pastry dough, then wrap the dough snuggly so that the cheese is entirely covered. Seal the seams with a touch of water.

5. Coat each cheese filled pastry wrap with an even, thin layer of vegetable oil over the surface of the pastry, to ensure a nice crisp fry.

6. Arrange the wrapped cheese rolls on the foil lined surface of the air fryer, side by side and not touching (you don't want the pastry to stick together as they expand).

7. Set the air fryer timer to 15 minutes.

8. After 15 minutes, the pastry crust should be golden brown and the cheese melted and perfect. Remove from the fryer basket with tongs and serve while hot.

NOTES:

Hooray for crispy pastry wrapped hot gooey cheese! This recipe will be a hit every time – nobody can say no to one of these little bites of heaven. Don't forget to serve with napkins. That crust is wonderfully flaky, and you don't want to lose a drop of that delicious hot cheese.

CREAMY ARTICHOKE SPINACH DIP

There is no greater party pleaser than a heaping dish of hot, creamy, cheesy spinach and artichoke dip. The air fryer gets a perfect crispy crust in the cheese on top, and this recipe hits just the right balance of vegetables to creamy base. Gather around your friends, family and guests, and treat them to this yummy favorite! *(Recipe serves 6-8 people.)*

INGREDIENTS:

½ cup of fresh or frozen spinach, steamed, drained and coarsely chopped

½ cup of fresh or canned artichoke hearts, drained and coarsely chopped

½ cup of milk

½ cup of cream cheese, softened

2 tablespoons of grated or powdered parmesan cheese

Pinch of salt and pepper

¼ cup of grated mozzarella cheese

INSTRUCTIONS:

1. Preheat the air fryer to 350 degrees.

2. In a mixing bowl, combine the milk, cream cheese, parmesan cheese, spinach, artichoke hearts, and salt and pepper. Mix thoroughly so that all ingredients are evenly combined, though no need to whip the mixture and risk pulverizing the artichoke hearts.

3. Pour the mixture into a heat safe 6-inch metal or ceramic baking dish, and sprinkle the grated mozzarella cheese over the top

4.   Set the air fryer timer to 20 minutes.

5.   After 20 minutes, when the air fryer shuts off, remove the baking dish using oven mitts and serve while warm.

NOTES:

Use warm pita bread, slices of toast, or your favorite cracker for dipping. Or, for an extra healthy snack, dip raw carrot or celery sticks into this creamy spinach artichoke goodness! Any way you try it, the crispy cheese topping will make this an absolutely delectable bite, which will hit the spot every time.

BACON WRAPPED PARTY WIENIES

Attention pork lovers, this appetizer is for you! The dynamic duo of crispy bacon and juicy hot cocktail wienies (or mini hot dogs, whatever you prefer – both work excellently) make these an all-time party favorite. *(Recipe serves 4-6 people.)*

INGREDIENTS:

8 small cocktail weenies or mini hot dogs

8 strips of thin sliced bacon

Pinch of salt and pepper

INSTRUCTIONS:

1.   Cover the basket of the air fryer with a lining of tin foil, leaving the edges uncovered to allow air to circulate through the basket.

2.   Preheat the air fryer to 350 degrees.

3.   One by one, wrap the bacon around the cocktail weenies, overlapping as you cover the length of the sausage.

4.   Lay each bacon wrapped weenie, seam side down, on the foil lined surface of the air fryer basket; all eight should fit snuggly without overlapping, though it's fine if the sides touch a little.

5.   Sprinkle the salt and pepper over the top of the wrapped weenies.

6.   Set the air fryer timer to 5 minutes.

7.   After five minutes, when the air fryer shuts off, turn each of the wrapped weenies over using tongs to ensure a nice even surface crisp.

8.   Reset the air fryer to 350 degrees for another 5 minutes.

9.   After 5 minutes, when the air fryer shuts off, the wrapped weenies will be succulent and perfect, and the bacon crisp and juicy
around them. Use tongs to place them on a plate and eat while
hot.

NOTES:

There is so much juicy, meaty goodness in each bite of these, that I prefer to enjoy them without any dipping sauce at all. Even so, if you've got
any, serve with a little spicy mustard on the side, as it complements the
flavors perfectly. Eat up and raise a glass to your delicious platter of
snacks!

CHEESY MUSHROOM BRUSCHETTA

Cheesy mushrooms on crisp toast is a gourmet snack that feels like comfort food in this fun twist on classic bruschetta. Kids and adults will appreciate this tasty appetizer treat.

INGREDIENTS:

½ cup of white or brown button mushrooms, washed, patted dry, and coarsely chopped

½ loaf of French bread or baguette

1 clove of fresh garlic, peeled and finely minced

3 ounces of sharp cheddar, sliced thick

1 tablespoon of extra virgin olive oil

Pinch of salt and pepper

INSTRUCTIONS:

1. Cover the basket of the air fryer with a lining of tin foil, leaving the edges uncovered to allow air to circulate through the basket.

2. Preheat the air fryer to 350 degrees.

3. In a mixing bowl, combine the mushrooms, olive oil, salt, pepper, and garlic. Stir thoroughly and set aside.

4. Cut the French bread into slices approximately 1inch thick – there should be 6-8 slices, depending on the bread.

5. Spoon some of the mushroom mixture onto each slice of bread, drizzling all over the surface, then top each piece with one of the cheddar slices.

6. Place the covered bread slices on the foil lined air fryer basket, evenly spaced – it's fine if the crusts are touching; they won't stick together thanks to the olive oil.

7. Set the air fryer timer to 15 minutes.

8. After 15 minutes, when the air fryer shuts off, remove the bruschetta with tongs and set on a serving plate. Enjoy while hot!

NOTES:

This may not sound like a natural dish for kids, but my children can't get enough of these crunchy, cheesy, gourmet open faced mushroom sandwiches (hey, "bruschetta" is a hard one for little kids to pronounce, even if they love to eat them!). This dish is also an excellent, vegetarian friendly appetizer for any elegant winter dinner party.

CRAB STUFFED MUSHROOM CAPS

These delectable little bites combine all the luxurious flavor of lump crab with the savory awesomeness of brown button mushrooms. These are a particularly elegant dish to serve at a cocktail party or to accompany a predinner drink, and will be sure to impress your friends, family or guests. *(Recipe serves 4-6 people.)*

INGREDIENTS:

½ cup of lump crab meat

1-2 medium sized brown button mushroom caps, rinsed and patted dry, stems removed

1 stalk of green onions, rinsed and minced

3 cloves of garlic, peeled and finely minced

1 tablespoon of mayonnaise

1 tablespoon of olive oil

¼ cup of breadcrumbs (Panko, or any other brand or homemade recipe)

Pinch of salt and pepper

INSTRUCTIONS:

1. Cover the basket of the air fryer with a lining of tin foil, leaving the edges uncovered to allow air to circulate through the basket.

2. Preheat the air fryer to 350 degrees.

3. Place the crab meat in a large mixing bowl, and mix in the mayonnaise, bread crumbs, onions, garlic, salt and pepper. Mix thoroughly, until all the ingredients are evenly combined.

4.   Lightly coat the mushroom caps with the olive oil. Spoon some of the crab mixture into each of the mushroom caps, overfilling each generously.

5.   Set the crab stuffed mushroom caps on the lined surface of the air fryer basket. Set the air fryer timer to 10 minutes.

6.   After 10 minutes, when the air fryer shuts off, remove the mushroom caps using tongs, and serve directly while hot.

NOTES:

These go great with a wedge of lemon served on the side for those who want to squeeze on a bit of juice for a tangy kick. These little bites are crispy on top and succulent and juicy in every bite. No matter how you serve them, this dish is pure deliciousness, and simple elegance to boot!

3

MAIN COURSES

CHICKEN

CHICKEN RANCH CHALUPA

This mouthwatering twist on the fried sandwich is a serious treat, for serious eaters. And thanks to the air fryer, the chicken will come out perfectly breaded and fried and the bacon crispy and delicious with zero added oil! Go ahead and indulge – this is the fried chicken sandwich of your dreams. *(Recipe serves 1-2 people.)*

INGREDIENTS:

6-inch premade flatbread dough (Pillsbury crust works great, or any homemade recipe)

1 medium sized white meat chicken breast, sliced and diced into bite sized pieces

1 cup of breadcrumbs (Panko brand works well)

2 medium sized eggs

Pinch of salt and pepper

2 teaspoon of ground rosemary

1 teaspoon of onion powder

3 strips of bacon

½ tablespoon of ranch sauce

INSTRUCTIONS:

1. Cover the basket of the air fryer with a lining of tin foil, leaving at least a ½inch edge uncovered to allow air to circulate. Preheat the air fryer to 360 degrees.

2. In a mixing bowl, beat the eggs until fluffy and until the yolks and whites are fully combined, and set aside.

3. In a separate mixing bowl, combine the breadcrumbs, onion powder, ground rosemary, and salt and pepper, and set aside.

4. One by one, dip each piece of raw chicken into the bowl with dry ingredients, coating all sides; then submerge into the egg bowl, then dip again into the dry ingredients. This double coating will ensure an extra crisp and delicious air fry!

5. Lay the coated chicken pieces on the foil covering the air fryer basket, in a single flat layer; this should take up approximately half the surface of the fryer basket.

6. On the other half of the fryer basket, lay the strips of bacon flat. Set the air fryer timer for 6 minutes.

7. After 6 minutes, the air fryer will turn off and the chicken should be midway cooked and the breaded coating starting to brown; the bacon should be cooked but not crisped.

8. Using tongs – careful not to burn your fingers! – turn each piece of bacon over, and flip the chicken as well to ensure a full allover fry.

9. Reset the air fryer to 360 degrees for another 6 minutes.

10. Roll the flatbread out, pierce several times with a fork to ensure even cooking, and spread the ranch sauce all over the surface.

11. After 6 minutes, when the air fryer shuts off, remove the bacon and chicken from the foil lined air fryer and layer them on the ranch smothered flatbread dough.

12. Fold the flatbread over so that all the meat is covered.

13. Using tongs, set the folded flatbread with the meat back onto the foil wrapped air fryer basket.

14. Set the air fryer to 350 degrees for five minutes.

15. After five minutes, when the air fryer shuts off, flip the flatbread – carefully, so as not to spill the fillings! – onto the other side.

16. Reset the air fryer to 350 degrees for another five minutes.

17. After five minutes, when the air fryer shuts off, remove the fried chalupa using tongs and set on a serving plate. The flatbread will be perfectly fried and golden brown, along with the crispy breaded chicken and perfectly done bacon, while the ranch will have kept those meats juicy and tender. Slice when cool – and enjoy!

NOTES:

This will fast become an all-time favorite for the whole family. There's just nothing more tantalizing than this juicy, crispy, chicken bacon ranch goodness. The fried crust will taste great dipped in a little extra ranch sauce, though the whole sandwich is so moist that it really doesn't need any extra treatment.

CHICKEN CHORIZO EMPANADAS

The combination of chicken and chorizo, with black olives and raisins for a touch of sweetness, wrapped in a crispy delicious empanada shell, is truly divine. This recipe takes a little extra time to prepare, but it's absolutely worth it. Best yet, the air fryer shaves considerable time off of conventional oven cooking and requires none of the added grease of deep fried empanadas. Use this recipe any time you really want to treat yourself and your family or friends. They'll love it, and so will you. *(Recipe serves 2-4 people.)*

INGREDIENTS:

4 ounces of white meat chicken breast, diced

4 ounces of chorizo sausage, removed from casings and crumbled

¼ cup of black olives, pitted and sliced

¼ cup of raises, white or black

4 premade empanada dough shells (preparation is chef's choice; Goya or Fargo both work well).

INSTRUCTIONS:

1. In a deep stovetop saucepan, sauté the chicken and the chorizo at medium heat. Add in the raisins, letting them plump in the oil naturally coming off the chorizo, stirring continuously with a wooden spoon, then add the olives. Break up the chorizo as it cooks, so it doesn't form large clumps.

2. Remove the saucepan from the stovetop as soon as the chicken is fully cooked. Do not overcook – you want the meat to remain

moist and juicy! Cover the saucepan and let stand on a heat safe surface for a few minutes.

3. Lay empanada shells flat on a clean counter.

4. Spoon the hot mixture from the saucepan into the empanada shells – a heaping spoonful on each, though not so much that the mixture spills over the edges.

5. Fold the empanada shells over so that the chicken and chorizo mixture is fully covered. Seal edges with water and press down with a fork to secure.

6. Cover the basket of the air fryer with a lining of tin foil, leaving at least a ½inch edge uncovered to allow air to circulate.

7. Place the empanadas in the foil lined air fryer basket and set at 350 degrees for 15 minutes.

8. Halfway through, slide the frying basket out and flip the empanadas using a spatula.

9. Remove when golden, and serve directly from the basket onto plates.

NOTES:

These succulent and luscious empanadas taste best when hot, with those juicy delicious meats mingling with the warm olives and plumped cooked raisins, but they'll work cold as well. Fully portable, and so satisfying, these are a wonderful treat when your lunch needs an extra kick. Enjoy!

MOZZARELLA CHICKEN STICKS

Cheesy chicken is one of my weaknesses. So, this recipe was created to satisfy an afternoon craving and it quickly became a family favorite. They are easy enough to throw together for a midday snack, but satisfying enough to eat as a full meal. Add a vegetable dish on the side and dinner is ready to go. (Serves 2-3 people.)

INGREDIENTS:

6 mozzarella sticks

1 cup flour

2 eggs

1 pound ground chicken

1 1/2 cups of breadcrumbs (Panko brand works well)

1/8 teaspoon Chili powder

1/8 teaspoon cayenne pepper

1/2 teaspoon garlic powder

1/4 teaspoon onion powder

1/2 teaspoon oregano

INSTRUCTIONS:

1. Cover the basket of the air fryer with a lining of tin foil, leaving the edges uncovered to allow air to circulate through the basket.

2. Preheat the air fryer to 390 degrees.

3. In a small bowl, mix together all of the seasonings.

4. In a mixing bowl combine the ground chicken and the spice mixture using a masher or your hands (if latter, be sure to wash thoroughly after handling raw meat!), until evenly combined.

5. In another mixing bowl, beat the eggs until fluffy and until the yolks and whites are fully combined, and set aside.

6. Pour the flour and the bread crumbs into two separate bowls. Place all four bowls within reach.

7. Take a mozzarella stick and cover it in the flour, then dunk it in the egg mixture. Use your hands to cover it in a thin layer of the ground chicken. Try to make the layer as even as possible to insure even cooking. Finally, coat the stick with the bread crumbs.

8. Repeat this for all the mozzarella sticks.

9. Place the mozzarella sticks in the air fryer in a single flat layer being sure that the sticks don't touch.

10. Set the air fryer for 10 minutes.

11. After 10 minutes, the air fryer will turn off and the mozzarella chicken sticks should be midway cooked and the breaded coating starting to brown.

12. Using tongs – careful not to burn your fingers! – turn each stick over to ensure a full allover fry.

13. Reset the timer for another 8 minutes.

14. When the air fryer shuts off remove the chicken sticks carefully with tongs and serve hot.

NOTES:

Although it hardly needs any dipping sauce, as the cheese is perfectly gooey and the chicken stays juicy, those who wish to indulge in dipping may enjoy warm marinara or ranch dressing.

CHEESY CHICKEN ASPARAGUS QUICHE

The nutrient rich, cruciferous asparagus is a delicacy in much of the world, and in this gorgeous savory quiche it's easy to see why. Combined with succulent chicken and a cheesy filling that will crisp perfectly in the air fryer, this quiche is a positively gourmet meal. *(Recipe serves 3-4 people.)*

INGREDIENTS:

Premade quiche crust, chilled and rolled flat to make a 6-inch pie crust (Pillsbury and Marie Callender's both offer great options, or feel free to use any other brand or homemade recipe).

2 eggs

¼ cup of milk

Pinch of salt and pepper

Medium sized, 5ounce breast of chicken, grilled and diced

½ cup of fresh asparagus, rinsed and patted dry, and sliced into bite sized pieces

¼ cup of shredded mozzarella cheese

¼ cup of shredded American cheese

INSTRUCTIONS:

1. Preheat the air fryer to 360 degrees.

2. Press the premade crust into a 6-inch pie tin, or any appropriately sized glass or ceramic heat safe dish. Press and trim at the edges if necessary.

3. With a fork, pierce several holes in the dough to allow air circulation and prevent cracking of the crust while cooking.

4. In a mixing bowl, beat the eggs until fluffy and until the yolks and white are evenly combined.

5. Add milk, asparagus, salt, pepper, chicken, and half the American and mozzarella cheese to the eggs.

6. Set the rest of the cheese aside for now, and stir the mixture until completely blended. Make sure the asparagus and chicken are spread evenly among the other ingredients.

7. Pour the mixture into the pie crust, slowly and carefully to avoid splashing. The mixture should almost fill the crust, but not completely – leaving a ¼ inch of crust at the edges.

8. Set the air fryer timer for 15 minutes.

9. After 15 minutes, the air fryer will shut off, and the quiche will already be firm and the crust beginning to brown. Sprinkle the rest of the American and mozzarella cheese on top of the quiche filling.

10. Reset the air fryer at 360 degrees for 5 minutes.

11. After 5 minutes, when the air fryer shuts off, the cheese will have formed an exquisite crust on top and the quiche will be golden brown and perfect. Remove from the air fryer using oven mitts or tongs, and set on a heat safe surface to cool for a few minutes before cutting.

NOTES:

This is a wonderful recipe to enjoy year round. It's hearty and warming for winter, and refreshing and light for summer when local asparagus might be in season. This filling meal should satisfy several people – try not to finish it all on your own, though it's so delicious it will be difficult not to!

AIR FRIED CHICKEN CHEESESTEAK

This recipe offers a wonderful twist on the classic Philly cheesesteak, with mushrooms to boot, and all that mouthwatering cheesy oniony fried goodness you want *without* all the added fat or grease of a regular fried sandwich. This sandwich is an all-out winner for those seeking decadence and health, all in one easy to prepare sandwich. *(Recipe serves 1-2 people.)*

INGREDIENTS:

Large hoagie bun, sliced in half

6-ounce white meat chicken breast, sliced into bite sized pieces

½ white onion, rinsed and sliced

¼ cup of white or brown button mushrooms, rinsed, patted dry and sliced

2 slices of American cheese

INSTRUCTIONS:

1.   Set the air fryer to 320 degrees for 10 minutes.

2.   Arrange the chicken pieces, onions and mushroom slices on a piece of tin foil trying to space the chicken so it is not overlapping the other ingredients. Set the tin foil on one side of the air fryer basket. The foil should not take up more than half of the surface. The juices from the chicken and the moisture from the mushrooms and onions will mingle while cooking – that's a good thing!

3.   Lay the hoagie bun halves, crusty side up and soft side down, on the other half of the air fryer.

4.   After 10 minutes, the air fryer will shut off; the hoagie buns should be starting to crisp and the chicken, mushrooms and onions will have begun to cook.

5.   Carefully – don't burn your fingers! – flip the hoagie buns so they are now crusty side down and soft side up; cover both sides with one slice each of American cheese.

6.   With a long spoon, gently stir the chicken, onion and mushrooms in the foil to ensure even coverage.

7.   Set the air fryer to 360 degrees for 6 minutes.

8.   After 6 minutes, when the fryer shuts off, the cheese will be perfectly melted over the toasted bread, and the chicken will be juicy on the inside and crispy on the outside.

9.   Remove the cheesy hoagie halves first, using tongs, and set on a serving plate; then cover one side with the chicken, and top with the onions and mushrooms. Close with the other cheesy hoagie half, slice into two pieces, and enjoy!

NOTES:

Feel free to add extra cheese, or cut out the mushrooms entirely, or however you like it. Little surprise, I always double the onions in the above recipe – crispy air fried and smothered in cheese, surrounded by mushrooms and chicken, it just doesn't get any better.

CHICKEN NACHO PIE

This original recipe is as much fun to prepare as it is to eat. It's perfect for parties or kids' sleepovers – an ideal meal to share with friends during good times. It's particularly fun because it's so easy to tailor and customize to your particular taste, a little more of this, a little less of that, maybe some guacamole for dipping. No matter what, this dinner will come out delicious. *(Recipe serves 3-4 people.)*

INGREDIENTS:

8 ounces of corn tortilla chips (any brand will do; I use Tostitos, mainly out of habit)

½ cup of grated cheddar cheese

½ cup of grated mozzarella cheese

4 ounces of white meat chicken breast, cooked and shredded

½ cup of medium salsa or

2 tablespoons of sour cream

INSTRUCTIONS:

1. Preheat air fryer to 320 degrees.

2. In a 6-inch heat safe pan or baking dish, arrange the tortilla chips. It's fine that they'll overlap. Add in half the grated cheddar and half the grated mozzarella, and shake the pan so the cheese is distributed.

3. Add the cooked, shredded chicken to the pan with the chips and the cheese, and then cover with the rest of the grated cheddar and mozzarella.

4.   Set the air fryer timer to 10 minutes.

5.   After 10 minutes, remove the baking dish with tongs or oven mitts. The tortilla chips will be lightly toasted, the chicken juicy and crispy, and the cheese perfectly melted.

6.   Top with sour cream and salsa, and serve while hot!

NOTES:

As I said, it's really easy to play with this recipe to taste. Sometimes I add slivers of jalapeño to the initial cheese sprinkle, for an extra spicy kick throughout the meal. If you don't have any guacamole on hand to pair with this, scallions in the sour cream also work really well as a substitute. Enjoy!

CHEESY CHICKEN TENDERS

This is an amazing recipe for any kids in your house or simply for your own inner child! Really, what kid doesn't get excited at the thought of delicious chicken tenders, moist and juicy on the inside and golden crispy brown on the outside. Combined with the parmesan cheese sprinkled through the breading, this is an irresistible twist on a beloved dinner classic. *(Recipe serves 3-4 people.)*

INGREDIENTS:

1 large white meat chicken breast, approximately 56 ounces, sliced into strips

1 cup of breadcrumbs (Panko brand works well)

2 medium sized eggs

Pinch of salt and pepper

1 tablespoon of grated or powdered parmesan cheese

INSTRUCTIONS:

1. Cover the basket of the air fryer with a lining of tin foil, leaving at least a ½inch space uncovered around the edges to allow air to circulate.

2. Preheat the air fryer to 350 degrees.

3. In a mixing bowl, beat the eggs until fluffy and until the yolks and whites are fully combined, and set aside.

4. In a separate mixing bowl, combine the breadcrumbs, parmesan, salt and pepper, and set aside.

5.   One by one, dip each piece of raw chicken into the bowl with dry ingredients, coating all sides; then submerge into the bowl with wet ingredients, then dip again into the dry ingredients. This double coating will ensure an extra crisp and delicious air fry!

6.   Lay the coated chicken pieces on the foil covering the air fryer basket, in a single flat layer.

7.   Set the air fryer timer for 15 minutes.

8.   After 15 minutes, the air fryer will turn off and the chicken should be midway cooked and the breaded coating starting to brown.

9.   Using tongs – careful not to burn your fingers! – turn each piece of chicken over to ensure a full allover fry.

10.   Reset the air fryer to 320 degrees for another 15 minutes.

11.   After 15 minutes, when the air fryer shuts off, remove the fried chicken strips using tongs and set on a serving plate. Eat as soon as cool enough to handle – and enjoy!

NOTES:

These chicken tenders are moist, juicy, tender, and – thanks to the air fried cheese crust – tasty enough to eat all on their own. Or, for those who like their dipping sauces, try honey mustard or ranch – you really can't go wrong; whatever you pair these chicken tenders with, they'll be a huge hit.

PERFECT CHICKEN PARMESAN

This traditional Italian favorite is perfectly adapted here for the air fryer, and comes out all the more delicious for it. The trick to a good chicken parm, of course, is a well crisped breaded crust on the chicken, and a gooey melt on the cheese. This recipe gets both just right and the air fryer makes it easy, with the result being a sumptuous iteration of this old classic. *Buon appetito! (Recipe serves 1-2 people.)*

INGREDIENTS:

2 large white meat chicken breasts, approximately 56 ounces

1 cup of breadcrumbs (Panko brand works well)

2 medium sized eggs

Pinch of salt and pepper

1 tablespoon of dried oregano

1 cup of marinara sauce (store-bought or homemade will do equally well)

2 slices of provolone cheese

1 tablespoon of parmesan cheese

INSTRUCTIONS:

1. Cover the basket of the air fryer with a lining of tin foil, leaving the edges uncovered to allow air to circulate through the basket.

2. Preheat the air fryer to 350 degrees.

3. In a mixing bowl, beat the eggs until fluffy and until the yolks and whites are fully combined, and set aside.

4. In a separate mixing bowl, combine the breadcrumbs, oregano, salt and pepper, and set aside.

5. One by one, dip the raw chicken breasts into the bowl with dry ingredients, coating both sides; then submerge into the bowl with wet ingredients, then dip again into the dry ingredients. This double coating will ensure an extra crisp and delicious air fry!

6. Lay the coated chicken breasts on the foil covering the air fryer basket, in a single flat layer.

7. Set the air fryer timer for 10 minutes.

8. After 10 minutes, the air fryer will turn off and the chicken should be midway cooked and the breaded coating starting to brown.

9. Using tongs – careful not to burn your fingers! – turn each piece of chicken over to ensure a full allover fry.

10. Reset the air fryer to 320 degrees for another 10 minutes.

11. While the chicken is cooking, pour half the marinara sauce into a 6-inch heat safe pan.

12. After 15 minutes, when the air fryer shuts off, remove the fried chicken breasts using tongs and set in the marinara covered pan. Drizzle the rest of the marinara sauce over the fried chicken, then place the slices of provolone cheese atop both of them and sprinkle the parmesan cheese over the entire pan.

13. Reset the air fryer to 350 degrees for 5 minutes.

14. After 5 minutes, when the air fryer shuts off, remove the dish from the air fryer using tongs or oven mitts. The chicken will be perfectly crisped and the cheese melted and lightly toasted. Serve while hot!

NOTES:

Classic Italian doesn't get easier or more perfect than this. This is an ideal meal for a romantic dinner for two, or the perfect reward for a long day at work. The best part is that there'll be plenty of cheesy sauce to mop up with some bread, or simply a spoon! Trust me, you won't want to leave a drop on your plate.

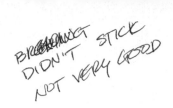
CHILI CHEESE AIR FRIED DRUMSTICKS

These tangy and juicy chicken drumsticks are the perfect dinner to serve at a family gathering, easy to eat finger food, with sauce that is literally finger lickin' good. The spicy chipotle kick will leave everyone fired up – in the good way – and the cheesy crust is just the thing to put a smile on everyone's faces. *(Recipe serves 3-4 people.)*

INGREDIENTS:

6 medium sized chicken drumsticks

1 raw egg

1 can of chipotle chilies packed in adobe sauce

2 tablespoons of grated cheddar cheese

½ cup of bread crumbs (I like Panko, but any brand or home recipe will do)

Pinch of salt and pepper

INSTRUCTIONS:

1. Cover the basket of the air fryer with a lining of tin foil, leaving the edges uncovered to allow air to circulate through the basket.

2. Preheat the air fryer to 350 degrees.

3. In a mixing bowl, beat the egg until fluffy and until the yolks and white are fully combined, and set aside.

4. In a blender or food processor, mince the chilies in the sauce fine enough so that they form a sort of paste. Add to the beaten egg, and with a whisk or a fork, combine thoroughly.

5. In a separate mixing bowl, combine the breadcrumbs, cheese, salt and pepper, and set aside.

6. One by one, dip the raw chicken drumsticks into the bowl with dry ingredients, coating all sides; then submerge into the bowl with wet ingredients, then dip again into the dry ingredients. This double coating will ensure an extra crisp and delicious air fry!

7. Lay the coated chicken drumsticks on the foil covering the air fryer basket, in a single flat layer.

8. Set the air fryer timer for 15 minutes.

9. After 15 minutes, the air fryer will turn off and the chicken should be midway cooked and the breaded coating starting to brown.

10. Using tongs – careful not to burn your fingers! – turn each chicken drumstick over to ensure a full allover fry.

11. Reset the air fryer to 300 degrees for 15 minutes.

12. After 15 minutes, when the air fryer shuts off, remove the fried chicken drumsticks using tongs and set on a serving plate. Eat as soon as cool enough to handle and enjoy!

NOTES:

Feel free to adjust the ratios of chilies to cheese in this recipe according to personal preference. In my family, we like our drumsticks extra spicy, but these work just as well if cooked with a heavier emphasis on the cheese. However you do them, eat up and enjoy! If you love a dipping sauce, try bleu cheese or ranch dressing.

TANDOORI CHICKEN MASALA

Oh, so you thought that just because you don't have a traditional tandoori oven in your home, that you needed to get takeout to enjoy this sumptuous Indian classic? Think again! This dish works so perfectly in the air fryer, with the chicken coming out tender and juicy and perfectly spiced and crisped. This dinner is sure to impress everyone and add a touch of the exotic to your repertoire. *(Recipe serves 2 people.)*

INGREDIENTS:

Two medium sized white meat chicken breasts, raw, and cut into bite sized chunks

½ cup of hung curd

1 teaspoon of turmeric powder

1 teaspoon of red chili powder

1 teaspoon of chicken masala powder

Pinch of salt

INSTRUCTIONS:

1. Preheat the air fryer to 350 degrees.

2. In a mixing bowl, combine the hung curd, turmeric, red chili powder, chicken masala powder, and salt. Stir until all ingredients are evenly combined, ensuring that the mixture is free of lumps.

3. Submerge all the pieces of chicken in the mixture, coating thoroughly; cover and refrigerate for 30 minutes to marinate.

4.   In a 6-inch heat safe pan, place the marinated chicken chunks and drizzle the rest of the marinade in the pan.

5.   Place the pan inside the air fryer basket (carefully, because it will be hot!), and set the air fryer timer to 25 minutes.

6.   After 25 minutes, when the fryer shuts off, the chicken will be perfectly cooked, juicy and spiced! Remove with tongs and serve while hot. Enjoy!

NOTES:

A little cucumber sauce on the side goes perfectly with this dish, or some mango chutney if you have it. However you eat them, once you try your air fried tandoori chicken, you'll never feel the need to order expensive takeout again. You've got your own Indian masala house right in your kitchen. Eat up and enjoy!

AIR FRYER CHICKEN

I certainly enjoy fried chicken, but not all the added grease and mess that accompanies frying it myself. I also don't appreciate all the fat that is added to my diet. Thanks to the air fryer I can indulge in air fried chicken that is just as delicious as any restaurant, but SO much healthier! (Serves 3 people.)

INGREDIENTS:

1 cup Louisiana Chicken Fry Seasoning, divided

3/4 cup water

1 1/2 pounds chicken legs, bone in (approximately 6 drumsticks)
Nonstick cooking spray

INSTRUCTIONS:

1. Cover the basket of the air fryer with a lining of tin foil, leaving the edges uncovered to allow air to circulate through the basket.

2. Preheat the air fryer to 360 degrees.

3. In a medium sized bowl, mix 1/2 cup of the Louisiana Chicken Fry Seasoning in with the water. Mix well to dissolve any lumps.

4. Place remaining 1/2 cup of the dry Louisiana Chicken Fry Seasoning in a shallow bowl.

5. One piece at a time, dip the chicken in the batter mixture. Then roll the chicken in the dry seasoning to coat. Finally, lightly spray the chicken with the cooking spray. Repeat with every piece of chicken.

6. Place the chicken in the air fryer in a single flat layer being sure that the pieces don't touch.

7.   Set the air fryer for 11 minutes.

8.   After 11 minutes, the air fryer will turn off and the chicken should be midway cooked and the breaded coating starting to brown.

9.   Using tongs – careful not to burn your fingers! – turn each piece over to ensure a full allover fry.

10.   Reset the timer for another 11 minutes.

11.   When the air fryer shuts off remove the chicken carefully with tongs as it will be hot!

NOTES:

It's always a good idea to check the internal temperature of the chicken before indulging as pieces that are different sizes may vary slightly in their cook time. Internal temperature should read 165 degrees Fahrenheit and juices should be clear.

BUFFALO FRIED CHICKEN WINGS

Everyone's game day favorite just went mainstream with this easy and delicious recipe that's simple to whip up any day of the year. I love the combination of tangy and spicy in this take on the classic buffalo wing, and nothing beats the crispy fried texture of the skin once it's finished. So, who cares if the Super Bowl is 11 months away? These wings don't need a special occasion to be the perfect dinner. *(Recipe serves 2-3 people.)*

INGREDIENTS:

8 medium sized chicken wings

½ cup of melted butter

2 tablespoons of hot sauce (Tabasco works great, or any brand will do)

½ tablespoon of vinegar

1 tablespoon of Worcestershire sauce

2 teaspoons of cayenne pepper

1 teaspoon of garlic powder

Pinch of salt and pepper

INSTRUCTIONS:

1. Cover the basket of the air fryer with a lining of tin foil, leaving the edges uncovered to allow air to circulate through the basket.

2. Preheat the air fryer to 350 degrees.

3. In a mixing bowl, combine the melted butter, hot sauce, vinegar, Worcestershire sauce, cayenne pepper, garlic powder, and salt and pepper.

4. Dunk the raw chicken wings into the mixture, coating thoroughly and allowing to marinate for at least 15 minutes.

5. Lay the coated chicken wings on the foil covering the air fryer basket, in a single flat layer.

6. Set the air fryer timer for 30 minutes.

7. Shake the air fryer handle several times during cooking, so the chicken wings jostle as they cook, ensuring an even surface crisp fry.

8. After 30 minutes, when the air fryer shuts off, remove the chicken wings using tongs and set on a serving plate. They should be crispy brown, moist and perfect. Eat as soon as cool enough to handle and enjoy!

NOTES:

The best pairing for this classic dinner is – what else? – fresh raw celery sticks and a nice bleu cheese or ranch dipping sauce. With or without a football game to watch while you eat, this dinner is a finger lickin' champion.

Beef, Pork and Lamb

Sugar and Spice Beef Empanadas

This is a mouthwatering meal for anyone who loves a touch of sweetness with their salty and savory foods. These empanadas get the balance just right, and with the air fryer they'll come out succulent and moist on the inside, and crispy crunch perfect on the outside, every single time. They're just as tasty when cool as when hot, and they're highly portable with no muss or fuss, making this a perfect recipe for when you are on the go. *(Recipe serves 2-4 people.)*

INGREDIENTS:

6 ounces of raw, lean ground beef

¼ cup of raw white onions, sliced and finely diced

1 teaspoon of cinnamon

½ teaspoon of nutmeg

½ teaspoon of ground cloves

1 small pinch of brown sugar

2 teaspoons of red chili powder

4 premade empanada dough shells (preparation is chef's choice; Goya or Fargo both work well).

INSTRUCTIONS:

1. In a deep stovetop saucepan, crumble and cook the ground beef at medium heat. Add in the onions, stirring continuously with a

wooden spoon, then add the cinnamon, nutmeg and cloves. Break up the ground beef as it cooks, so it doesn't form large clumps.

2. Remove the saucepan from the stovetop as soon as the beef is fully cooked, the onions are soft, and the spices are releasing their fragrances. Do not overcook. You want the meat to remain moist and juicy! Cover the saucepan and let stand on a heat safe surface for a few minutes.

3. Lay empanada shells flat on a clean counter.

4. Spoon the spiced cooked beef from the saucepan into the empanada shells – a heaping spoonful on each, though not so much that the mixture spills over the edges.

5. Fold the empanada shells over so that the spiced beef is fully covered. Seal edges with water and press down with a fork to secure.

6. Sprinkle brown sugar over the still wet seams of the empanadas, for an extra sweet crunch.

7. Cover the basket of the air fryer with a lining of tin foil, leaving at least a ½inch edge uncovered to allow air to circulate.

8. Place the empanadas in the foil lined air fryer basket and set at 350 degrees for 15 minutes.

9. Halfway through, slide the frying basket out and flip the empanadas using a spatula.

10. Remove when golden, and serve directly from the basket onto plates.

NOTES:

These awesome empanadas will keep their crunch and flavor just fine once cooled, so don't think twice about wrapping them in some tin foil and taking them with you on the go. Hot or cold, the shells will be crispy and delicious, and the spiced beef will be succulent and juicy. Enjoy any-time, anywhere!

CHICKEN FRIED STEAK AND ONION FLATBREAD

Ok, get ready to start salivating! I start getting hungry just *thinking* about this amazing sandwich. The combination of juicy, crunchy chicken fried steak with crispy fried onions is just irresistible, and the Swiss cheese topping is perfection. The best part? It's got none of the added fat or oil that you'd normally need to chicken fry a steak. Enjoy! *(Recipe serves 1-2 people.)*

INGREDIENTS:

6-inch premade flatbread dough (Pillsbury crust works great, or any homemade recipe)

1 medium sized sirloin or flank steak, sliced and diced into bite sized pieces

2 cups of breadcrumbs (Panko brand works well)

2 medium sized eggs

Pinch of salt and pepper

2 teaspoons of onion powder

½ a medium sized white onion, rinsed and sliced

2 medium sized slices of Swiss cheese

INSTRUCTIONS:

1. Cover the basket of the air fryer with a lining of tin foil, leaving at least a ½inch edge uncovered to allow air to circulate.

2. Preheat the air fryer to 360 degrees.

3. In a mixing bowl, beat the eggs until fluffy and until the yolks and whites are fully combined, and set aside.

4. In a separate mixing bowl, combine the breadcrumbs, onion powder, and salt and pepper, and set aside.

5. One by one, dip each piece of raw steak into the bowl with dry ingredients, coating all sides. Then submerge into the bowl with the eggs, then dip again into the dry ingredients. This double coating will ensure an extra crisp and delicious air fry!

6. Lay the coated steak pieces on the foil covering the air fryer basket, in a single flat layer; this should take up approximately half the surface of the fryer basket.

7. On the other half of the fryer basket, lay the onion slices.

8. Set the air fryer timer for 6 minutes.

9. After 6 minutes, the air fryer will turn off and the steak should be midway cooked and the breaded coating starting to brown; the onions should be starting to crisp.

10. Using tongs – careful not to burn your fingers! – turn over the onions, and flip the steak pieces as well to ensure a full allover fry.

11. Reset the air fryer to 360 degrees for another 6 minutes.

12. Roll the flatbread out, pierce several times with a fork to ensure even cooking, and lay the slices of Swiss cheese on the surface.

13. After 6 minutes, when the air fryer shuts off, remove the onions and steak from the foil lined air fryer and layer them on the cheese covered flatbread dough.

14. Fold the flatbread over so that all the meat is covered.

15. Using tongs, set the folded flatbread with the meat, onions and cheese back onto the foil wrapped air fryer basket.

16. Set the air fryer to 350 degrees for five minutes.

17. After five minutes, when the air fryer shuts off, flip the flatbread – carefully, so as not to spill the fillings! – onto the other side.

18. Reset the air fryer to 350 degrees for another five minutes.

19. After five minutes, when the air fryer shuts off, remove using tongs and set on a serving plate. The flatbread will be perfectly fried and golden brown, along with the crunchy breaded steak and perfectly crispy onions, while the cheese will have melted and kept the meat juicy and tender. Slice when cool – and enjoy!

NOTES:

This drool worthy dish is especially welcome in those cold winter months when you need a hearty meal that will really satisfy you and warm you up. I like to throw extra onion into the recipe – usually a whole medium sized onion – but feel free to experiment. This sandwich will taste impeccable every time!

MEAT LOVERS' PIZZA

Herbivores, beware! This recipe packs the meaty triple punch of pepperoni, steak, and sweet Italian sausage – an absolute fantasy come true for anyone craving a filling and delicious pizza dish. And, thanks to your air fryer, this treat comes with absolutely zero added fat or grease. That may sound like a dream come true, but you better believe it, because meat lovers, this pizza is for you! *(Recipe serves 1-2 people.)*

INGREDIENTS:

1 pre-prepared 6-inch pizza pie crust (Mama Mary and Patty's Gourmet Pizza both make great versions, or feel free to use the brand of your choice or a homemade preparation), defrosted if necessary.

1/3 cup of marinara sauce – a personal recipe is fine, or any store-bought brand will do.

2 ounces of grilled steak, sliced into bite sized pieces

2 ounces of salami, sliced fine

2 ounces of pepperoni, sliced fine

¼ cup of American cheese

¼ cup of shredded mozzarella cheese

INSTRUCTIONS:

1. Preheat the air fryer to 350 degrees.

2. Lay the pizza dough flat on a sheet of parchment paper or tin foil, cut large enough to hold the entire pie crust, but small enough that it will leave the edges of the air frying basket uncovered to allow for air circulation.

3.   Using a fork, stab the pizza dough several times across the surface – piercing the pie crust will allow air to circulate throughout the crust and ensure even cooking.

4.   With a deep soup spoon, ladle the marinara sauce onto the pizza dough, and spread evenly in expanding circles over the surface of the piecrust. Be sure to leave at least ½ inch of bare dough around the edges, to ensure that extra crispy crunchy first bite of the crust!

5.   Distribute the pieces of steak and the slices of salami and pepperoni evenly over the sauce covered dough, then sprinkle the cheese in an even layer on top.

6.   Set the air fryer timer to 1-2 minutes, and place the pizza with foil or paper on the fryer's basket surface. Again, be sure to leave the edges of the basket uncovered to allow for proper air circulation, and don't let your bare fingers touch the hot surface!

7.   After 1-2 minutes, when the air fryer shuts off, the cheese should be perfectly melted and lightly crisped, and the pie crust should be golden brown.

8.   Using a spatula – or two, if necessary! – remove the pizza from the air fryer basket and set on a serving plate. Wait a few minutes until the pie is cool enough to handle, then cut into slices and serve.

NOTES:

Meaty, cheesy, gooey in the center and crispy and perfect on the outside pizza just doesn't get any better than this. This pizza is filling enough to share and everyone will be begging for a slice. Its also good enough to hoard all for yourself. Dig in and enjoy!

AIR FRIED PHILLY CHEESESTEAK

Think you need to fly to eastern Pennsylvania to enjoy a juicy, crispy, gooey cheesesteak? Think again! This recipe gets the most delicious results, with none of the downside and it couldn't be more simple! Sorry Philadelphia, *this* cheesesteak is simply the best. *(Recipe serves 1-2 people.)*

INGREDIENTS:

Large hoagie bun, sliced in half

6 ounces of sirloin or flank steak, sliced into bite sized pieces

½ white onion, rinsed and sliced

½ red pepper, rinsed and sliced

2 slices of American cheese

INSTRUCTIONS:

1. Set the air fryer to 320 degrees.

2. Arrange the steak pieces, onions and peppers on a piece of tin foil, flat and not overlapping, and set the tin foil on one side of the air fryer basket. The foil should not take up more than half of the surface; the juices from the steak and the moisture from the vegetables will mingle while cooking – that's a good thing!

3. Lay the hoagie bun halves, crusty side up and soft side down, on the other half of the air fryer. Set the timer for 10 minutes.

4. After 10 minutes, the air fryer will shut off. The hoagie buns should be starting to crisp and the steak and vegetables will have begun to cook.

5. Carefully – don't burn your fingers! – flip the hoagie buns so they are now crusty side down and soft side up; cover both sides with one slice each of American cheese.

6. With a long spoon, gently stir the steak, onions and peppers in the foil to ensure even coverage.

7. Set the air fryer to 360 degrees for 6 minutes.

8. After 6 minutes, when the fryer shuts off, the cheese will be perfectly melted over the toasted bread, and the steak will be juicy on the inside and crispy on the outside.

9. Remove the cheesy hoagie halves first, using tongs, and set on a serving plate. Then cover one side with the steak, and top with the onions and peppers. Close with the other cheesy hoagie half, slice into two pieces, and enjoy!

NOTES:

Feel free to add extra cheese, or cut the peppers entirely, or however you would order your cheesesteak if you *were* in Philadelphia.

RUEBEN SANDWICH SPRING ROLLS

Any Rueben lovers out there will appreciate this twist on the classic sandwich that makes it easily portable and fun! By inclosing the sauerkraut in the spring roll wrapper, it lessens the likelihood that you will find sauerkraut in your lap though I make no promises! The air fryer insures a perfectly crisp spring roll filled with melty cheese and warm corned beef. Just add Thousand Island dressing and your "sandwich" experience is complete. (Serves 4-5 people.)

INGREDIENTS:

10 spring roll wrappers (any brand will do, we like Blue Dragon or Tasty Joy, both available through Target or Walmart, or any large grocery chain)

1/3 pound of corned beef (pastrami cut into strips will work, too)

5 slices of swiss cheese, cut up into strips

2 cups sauerkraut, drained and squeezed dry

1 egg

1 teaspoon of corn starch

Thousand Island Dressing for dipping

INSTRUCTIONS:

1. Cover the basket of the air fryer with a lining of tin foil, leaving the edges uncovered to allow air to circulate through the basket.

2. Preheat the air fryer to 360 degrees.

3. In a small bowl, beat the egg until fluffy and until the yolk and white are combined. Add the cornstarch and mix until the ingredients thicken. Set aside.

4. Lay out the spring roll wrappers in a diamond shape on a dry, clean surface. In the middle, place a few strips of the cut up corned beef.

5. Add a few strips of swiss cheese and top with 1-2 tablespoons of sauerkraut.

6. Roll up and seal the seams with the egg and cornstarch mixture.

7. Place each roll on the foil lined air fryer basket.

8. Set the air fryer timer to 7 minutes. During cooking, shake the handle of the fryer basket several times to ensure a nice even surface crisp.

9. After 7 minutes, when the air fryer shuts off, the spring rolls should be golden brown and perfect. Remove with tongs and serve while hot with a side of Thousand Island for dipping.

NOTES:

I've found that wrapping any sandwich ingredients in spring roll wrappers makes even the pickiest eaters excited about mealtime. Get creative and try your favorite sandwich toppings in a roll. Somehow it just makes eating more fun!

CHICKEN FRIED STEAK SUPREME

This hearty, savory recipe offers a delicious and protein packed dinner, with none of the added grease or oil that you'd normally need to make good chicken fried steak. The touch of thyme in this version of the beefy classic adds a wonderful savory twist, and the air fryer ensures the steak stays tender and juicy inside its perfect crispy crust. *(Recipe serves 1-2 people.)*

INGREDIENTS:

½ pound beef bottom round, sliced into strips

1 cup of breadcrumbs (Panko brand works well)

2 medium sized eggs

Pinch of salt and pepper

½ tablespoon of ground thyme

INSTRUCTIONS:

1. Cover the basket of the air fryer with a lining of tin foil, leaving the edges uncovered to allow air to circulate through the basket.

2. Preheat the air fryer to 350 degrees.

3. In a mixing bowl, beat the eggs until fluffy and until the yolks and whites are fully combined, and set aside.

4. In a separate mixing bowl, combine the breadcrumbs, thyme, salt and pepper, and set aside.

5. One by one, dip each piece of raw steak into the bowl with dry ingredients, coating all sides; then submerge into the bowl with

wet ingredients, then dip again into the dry ingredients. This double coating will ensure an extra crisp and delicious air fry!

6. Lay the coated steak pieces on the foil covering the air fryer basket, in a single flat layer.

7. Set the air fryer timer for 15 minutes.

8. After 15 minutes, the air fryer will turn off and the steak should be midway cooked and the breaded coating starting to brown.

9. Using tongs – careful not to burn your fingers! – turn each piece of steak over to ensure a full allover fry.

10. Reset the air fryer to 320 degrees for 15 minutes.

11. After 15 minutes, when the air fryer shuts off, remove the fried steak strips using tongs and set on a serving plate. Eat as soon as cool enough to handle and enjoy!

NOTES:

These chicken fried steak strips go wonderfully with your favorite hot gravy or with any dipping sauce you like. I enjoy ranch! A fresh salad on the side is a good pairing, resulting in a perfectly balanced, and mouth-wateringly delicious dinner.

WORLD'S GREATEST BEEF BURGER

It's a tall claim, I know, but I honestly believe this recipe backs it up 100%. The combination of salty soy sauce with tangy sweet ketchup is a well-kept secret to turn ordinary ground beef into heavenly hamburgers. Keep this recipe close – and only share with trust friends! No need for *everyone* to know the secret for the world's greatest beef burger. *(Recipe serves 2 people.)*

INGREDIENTS:

1 cup of raw ground beef, or 8 ounces

1 ½ tablespoons of ketchup

1 ½ tablespoons of soy sauce

Pinch of salt and pepper

INSTRUCTIONS:

1. Cover the basket of the air fryer with a lining of tin foil, leaving the edges uncovered to allow air to circulate through the basket.

2. Preheat the air fryer to 350 degrees.

3. In a mixing bowl, combine the meat, ketchup, soy sauce, salt and pepper, using a masher or your hands (if latter, be sure to wash thoroughly after handling raw meat!), until evenly combined.

4. When the combination is evenly mixed, divide and shape into two separate patties, then place on the foil covered air fryer basket. (Careful, because the device will be hot!)

5. Set the air fryer timer for 10 minutes.

6. After 10 minutes, the air fryer will turn off and the patties should be starting to brown.

7. Using tongs – careful not to burn your fingers! – turn each patty over to ensure a full allover fry.

8. Reset the air fryer to 300 degrees for 10 minutes.

9. After 10 minutes, when the air fryer shuts off, remove the burgers using tongs and set on a serving plate.

NOTES:

If you like cheese on your burger, place a slice of American on each patty directly after it comes off the air fryer; the meat will still be hot enough to melt the cheese. Serve with hamburger buns and condiments according to personal preferences. I like onions, tomato, and a little mustard. However you like your burger, dig in and enjoy the meaty goodness.

FRIED PORK QUESADILLA

This recipe is a scrumptious twist on the classic quesadilla, with savory braised pork that is as healthy as it is delicious. I love the addition of peppers and onions in this Mexicali treat – and of course tons of cheese! With this quesadilla on the menu, meals will be anything but boring. *(Recipe serves 1-2 people.)*

INGREDIENTS:

Two 6-inch corn or flour tortilla shells

1 medium sized pork shoulder, approximately 4 ounces, sliced

½ medium sized white onion, sliced

½ medium sized red pepper, sliced

½ medium sized green pepper, sliced

½ medium sized yellow pepper, sliced

¼ cup of shredded pepper jack cheese

¼ cup of shredded mozzarella cheese

INSTRUCTIONS:

1. Preheat the air fryer to 350 degrees.

2. In the oven on high heat for 20 minutes, grill the pork, onion, and peppers in foil in the same pan, allowing the moisture from the vegetables and the juice from the pork mingle together.

3. Remove pork and vegetables in foil from the oven. While they're cooling, sprinkle half the shredded cheese over one of the tortillas, then cover with the pieces of pork, onions, and peppers, and

then layer on the rest of the shredded cheese. Top with the second tortilla.

4. Place directly on hot surface of the air frying basket, but be careful not to burn your fingers!

5. Set air fryer timer for 6 minutes.

6. After 6 minutes, when the air fryer shuts off, flip the tortillas onto the other side with a spatula; the cheese should be melted enough that it won't fall apart, but be careful anyway not to spill any toppings!

7. Reset air fryer to 350 degrees for another 6 minutes.

8. After 6 minutes, when the air fryer shuts off, the tortillas should be browned and crisp, and the pork, onion, peppers and cheese will be crispy and hot and delicious. Remove with tongs and let sit on a serving plate to cool for a few minutes before slicing.

NOTES:

This lunch goes great with a little salsa and sour cream on the side, or even guacamole if you've got some. But truly, it's just perfect all on its own – so perfect, you'll be hesitant to share it, though everyone around you will be begging for a slice! Eat up and enjoy while you've got it all to yourself – or whip up another fast and easy batch to share!

SUPREME FRIED HAM AND CHEESE SANDWICH

This recipe packs the ultimate comfort food into one gooey, delicious fried sandwich. With hot cheese and succulent air fried ham, lunch couldn't be any more delicious. Even better, you're dealing with a tiny fraction of the butter that you would normally need for a good fried ham and cheese sandwich. *(Recipe serves 2 people.)*

INGREDIENTS:

4 slices of white bread

2 slices of premium cheddar cheese

2 slices of provolone cheese

4 slices of premium baked or smoked ham

1 small pat of butter

INSTRUCTIONS:

1. Preheat the air fryer to 360 degrees.

2. Lightly spread the butter on both sides of each slice of bread – and I do mean lightly! You don't need more than a very thin coat on each side.

3. Lay the slices of bread on the air frying basket; side by side, they should fit snuggly, with the edges barely touching (it's fine if they do, as long as they don't overlap).

4. Set the air fryer timer to 6 minutes.

5. After 6 minutes, when the air fryer shuts off, the bread should be beginning to crisp and brown. Using a spatula, flip over each slice of bread.

6. Cover two of the bread slices with a layer of cheddar cheese, and the other two slices with a layer of the provolone and then the ham.

7. Set the air fryer to 320 degrees for 10 minutes.

8. After 10 minutes, when the air fryer shuts off, the cheeses should be melted and lightly bubbling, the ham should be starting to crisp, and the bread should be perfectly toasted to a golden brown.

9. Using a spatula, place the ham and provolone covered bread slices on a serving plate, and top each with the cheddar covered slices.

10. Slice in half once cool enough to handle, and serve with a side of soup, salad, or – most likely – a second helping!

NOTES:

This sandwich is best enjoyed while hot, though it's also fine to wrap up in foil to enjoy later. Just makes sure the cheese has cooled down and bring a napkin!

FRIED PORK SCOTCH EGG

This amazing dish is traditional in parts of the U.K., and you can even find them ready made in some grocery stores. But nothing beats this perfect homemade recipe – savory fried pork, soft boiled egg, crunchy crispy breaded crust...it's impossible not to fall in love! *(Recipe serves 2-3 people.)*

INGREDIENTS:

3 soft boiled eggs, peeled

8 ounces of raw minced pork, or sausage outside the casings

2 teaspoons of ground rosemary

2 teaspoons of garlic powder

Pinch of salt and pepper

2 raw eggs

1 cup of breadcrumbs (I like Panko, but other brands are fine, or home-made bread crumbs work too)

INSTRUCTIONS:

1. Cover the basket of the air fryer with a lining of tin foil, leaving the edges uncovered to allow air to circulate through the basket.

2. Preheat the air fryer to 350 degrees.

3. In a mixing bowl, combine the raw pork with the rosemary, garlic powder, salt and pepper. This will probably be easiest to do with your masher or bare hands (though make sure to wash thoroughly after handling raw meat!) Combine until all the spices are evenly spread throughout the meat.

4. Divide the meat mixture into three equal portions in the mixing bowl, and form each into balls with your hands.

5. Lay a large sheet of plastic wrap on the countertop, and flatten one of the balls of meat on top of it, to form a wide, flat meat circle.

6. Place one of the peeled soft boiled eggs in the center of the meat circle and then, using the ends of the plastic wrap, pull the meat circle so that it is fully covering and surrounding the soft-boiled egg.

7. Tighten and shape the plastic wrap covering the meat so that if forms a ball, and make sure not to squeeze too hard lest you squish the soft-boiled egg at the center of the ball! Set aside.

8. Repeat steps 57 with the other two soft-boiled eggs and portions of meat mixture.

9. In a separate mixing bowl, beat the two raw eggs until fluffy and until the yolks and whites are fully combined.

10. One by one, remove the plastic wrap and dunk the pork covered balls into the raw egg mixture, and then roll them in the bread crumbs, covering fully and generously.

11. Place each of the breadcrumb covered, meat wrapped balls onto the foil lined surface of the air fryer. Three of them should fit nicely, without touching.

12. Set the air fryer timer to 25 minutes.

13. About halfway through the cooking time, shake the handle of the air fryer vigorously, so that the scotch eggs inside roll around and ensure full coverage.

14. After 25 minutes, the air fryer will shut off and the scotch eggs should be perfect. The meat should be fully cooked, the egg yolks still runny on the inside, and the outsides crispy and golden brown. Using tongs, place them on serving plates, slice in half, and enjoy!

NOTES:

These delicious treats go perfectly dipped in a little spicy mustard, or all alone. They're also great to wrap up and enjoy for dinner on the go. However you eat them, this is a filling and delightful dinner that every-one will love.

MARINATED PORK MEDALLIONS

These pork medallions are so easy to pull together, but they take a bit of planning ahead. Make your marinade and toss in the medallions a few days before you have a busy evening. On that busy night, you will be so glad to have a wholesome meal to serve your family! (Serves 3-4 people.)

INGREDIENTS:

1 pound pork tenderloin, cut into 8 equal size medallions

1 cup soy sauce

1/2 cup olive oil

3 cloves garlic, crushed

1 teaspoon fresh grated ginger

1 tablespoon brown sugar

Nonstick cooking spray

INSTRUCTIONS:

1. In a small bowl, mix together all of the ingredients except for the pork and the cooking spray. Pour ingredients into a resealable bag. Place the pork medallions in the bag and place in the fridge to marinate for up to two days.

2. When ready to cook, cover the basket of the air fryer with a lining of tin foil, leaving the edges uncovered to allow air to circulate through the basket. Spray the foil lightly with nonstick cooking spray.

3. Preheat the air fryer to 360 degrees.

4. Remove pork medallions from the marinade and discard the marinade. Place medallions in the air fryer basket in rows. The medallions can be touching but not overlapping.

5. Set the air fryer for 10 minutes.

6. After 10 minutes, when the air fryer shuts off the medallions should be cooked through and juicy. Remove with tongs and serve immediately while hot!

NOTES:

With a side salad and a baked potato this makes an easy, but delicious weeknight meal. Marinating the pork makes it tender and succulent and the air fryer roasts it perfectly.

MINTY CHICKEN FRIED PORK CHOPS

Is there any more inviting dinner than crispy fried pork chops? The meat tender and juicy, the surface crunchy and golden delicious. This dinner is a consistent hit, and best of all, with the air fryer it's quite healthy. The hint of mint in this recipe adds a truly delicious zing, and adds a touch of the unexpected to this classic dish. *(Recipe serves 3-4 people.)*

INGREDIENTS:

4 medium sized pork chops, approximately 3.5 ounces each

1 cup of breadcrumbs (Panko brand works well)

2 medium sized eggs

Pinch of salt and pepper

½ tablespoon of mint, either dried and ground; or fresh, rinsed, and finely chopped

INSTRUCTIONS:

1. Cover the basket of the air fryer with a lining of tin foil, leaving the edges uncovered to allow air to circulate through the basket.

2. Preheat the air fryer to 350 degrees.

3. In a mixing bowl, beat the eggs until fluffy and until the yolks and whites are fully combined, and set aside.

4. In a separate mixing bowl, combine the breadcrumbs, mint, salt and pepper, and set aside.

5. One by one, dip each raw pork chop into the bowl with dry in-gredients, coating all sides. Then submerge into the bowl with

wet ingredients, then dip again into the dry ingredients. This double coating will ensure an extra crisp and delicious air fry!

6. Lay the coated pork chops on the foil covering the air fryer basket, in a single flat layer.

7. Set the air fryer timer for 15 minutes.

8. After 15 minutes, the air fryer will turn off and the pork should be midway cooked and the breaded coating starting to brown.

9. Using tongs – careful not to burn your fingers! – turn each piece of pork over to ensure a full allover fry.

10. Reset the air fryer to 320 degrees for 15 minutes.

11. After 15 minutes, when the air fryer shuts off, remove the fried pork chops using tongs and set on a serving plate. Eat as soon as cool enough to handle and enjoy!

NOTES:

These awesome pork chops go terrific with a little bit of applesauce on the side, or a bit of mint jelly, a popular pork pairing in England. Some greens on the side or a salad is the perfect addition to make this a healthy, balanced, and delicious dinner. Enjoy!

SPICED LAMB SAMOSAS

This is a meaty twist on the vegetarian Indian classic, an absolutely mouthwatering dish with enough lean protein to power you through until your next meal. Along with being healthy and delicious, this recipe is also extremely easy to make and even easier to transport. What more could you ask for in quick and yummy dish? *(Recipe serves 2-3 people.)*

INGREDIENTS:

6 ounces of ground lamb, minced and sautéed

¼ cup of green peas, boiled and rinsed

½ a medium sized white onion, finely minced and steamed

1 teaspoon of garam masala powder

½ teaspoon of ginger garlic paste

½ teaspoon of red chili powder

½ teaspoon of turmeric powder

Pinch of salt and pepper

3 sheets of flaky puff pastry dough (Pillsbury makes an excellent version, or any other brand or home recipe will do fine)

INSTRUCTIONS:

1. Preheat air fryer to 350 degrees.

2. In a mixing bowl, mix the ground lamb with the garam masala powder, ginger garlic paste, red chili powder, turmeric powder, and salt and pepper.

3. Add in the peas and onion, and stir entire mixture together until ingredients are evenly blended.

4.   Divide the mixture into three equal segments.

5.   Lay the sheets of puff pastry dough flat on a clean surface.

6.   Fill each sheet of dough with one of the three portions of lamb mix, then fold the pastry over into a triangle, so it neatly tucks and covers the meat. Seal the edges with a bit of water.

7.   Place the three samosas directly in the air fryer basket. Set the air fryer timer to 6 minutes.

8.   After 5 minutes, when the fryer shuts off, use tongs to flip the samosas over.

9.   Reset the air fryer at 350 degrees for another 6 minutes.

10. After six minutes, when the air fryer shuts off, the samosas will be perfect – hot and juicy on the inside, crispy and flaky and perfectly fried on the outside. Remove with tongs, and set to cool for a few minutes before digging in!

NOTES:

A little mango chutney or cucumber sauce goes a long way with these samosas, though they're also perfect on their own. And don't forget, each samosa is a complete balanced meal all by itself – so enjoy knowing that, as yummy as it tastes, it's also doing your body good. Dig in!

SAVORY BREADED LAMB CHOPS

This recipe for scrumptious breaded lamb is absolutely perfect. Thanks to the air fryer, the lamb will remain tender and juicy on the inside, and perfectly crisped with a rich and savory crust on the outside. I love this seasoning combination and I adore how the meat is perfectly marinated in spices while it's cooking. So easy...so delicious! *(Recipe serves 2-3 people.)*

INGREDIENTS:

Three medium sized lamb chops, about 3.5 ounces each

1 cup of breadcrumbs (Panko brand works well)

2 medium sized eggs

Pinch of salt and pepper

½ tablespoon of ground thyme

½ teaspoon of garlic powder

½ teaspoon of ground rosemary

½ teaspoon of cayenne powder

INSTRUCTIONS:

1. Cover the basket of the air fryer with a lining of tin foil, leaving the edges uncovered to allow air to circulate through the basket.

2. Preheat the air fryer to 350 degrees.

3. In a mixing bowl, beat the eggs until fluffy and until the yolks and whites are fully combined, and set aside.

4. In a separate mixing bowl, combine the breadcrumbs, thyme, garlic, rosemary, cayenne, salt, and pepper, and set aside.

5. One by one, dip each lamb chop into the bowl with dry ingredients, coating all sides Then submerge into the bowl with wet ingredients, then dip again into the dry ingredients. This double coating will ensure an extra crisp and delicious air fry!

6. Lay the coated lamb chops on the foil covering the air fryer basket, in a single flat layer.

7. Set the air fryer timer for 15 minutes.

8. After 15 minutes, the air fryer will turn off and the lamb should be midway cooked and the breaded coating starting to brown.

9. Using tongs – careful not to burn your fingers! – turn each lamb chop over to ensure a full allover fry.

10. Reset the air fryer to 320 degrees for 15 minutes.

11. After 15 minutes, when the air fryer shuts off, remove the fried lamb chops using tongs and set on a serving plate. Eat as soon as cool enough to handle and enjoy!

NOTES:

This is the perfect dinner for a cold winter night, and absolutely one of the tastiest ways to enjoy lamb. So juicy and tender you'll hardly need any gravy or dipping sauce, though any flavor will work great if you prefer some kind of addition. A side salad or some fresh green beans are also a great veggie pairing for a complete and balanced meal.

SEAFOOD

OPEN FACED SUPER TUNA MELT

This is a terrific sandwich that's both healthy and hearty, perfect for those days when you need your lunch to fill you up without weighing you down. In this recipe, the classic tuna melt gets a twist with onions and tomatoes, making this a complete and balanced meal on its own. *(Recipe serves 3-4 people.)*

INGREDIENTS:

4 slices of white bread

1-2ounce can of tuna fish, drained

1-2 tablespoon of mayonnaise

Pinch of salt and pepper

½ white onion, finely sliced

1 medium sized red tomato, sliced

4 slices of cheddar cheese

1 small pat of butter

INSTRUCTIONS:

1. Preheat the air fryer to 360 degrees.

2. Lightly spread the butter on both sides of each slice of bread – and I do mean lightly! You don't need more than a very thin coat on each side.

3. Lay the slices of bread on the air frying basket; side by side, they should fit snuggly, with the edges barely touching (it's fine if they do, as long as they don't overlap).

4. Set the air fryer timer to 6 minutes.

5. While the bread is toasting in the air fryer, combine the tuna fish, salt and pepper, and mayonnaise in a small mixing bowl, mixing so they are evenly blended.

6. After 6 minutes, when the air fryer shuts off, the bread should be beginning to crisp and brown. Using a spatula, flip over each slice of bread.

7. Cover each slice of bread with a large spoonful of the tuna mayonnaise mixture, spread evenly, then cover each with a few slices of tomato, onion, and – last but not least! – the cheddar cheese.

8. Set the air fryer to 320 degrees for 10 minutes.

9. After 10 minutes, when the air fryer shuts off, the cheese should be melted and lightly bubbling, the bread should be perfectly toasted to a golden brown, the onions crispy and delicious and the tomatoes juicy. Add salt and pepper to taste.

10. Using a spatula, place each slice on a serving plate. Either enjoy open faced, or close the sides and slice in half to make giant tuna melt sandwiches!

NOTES:

Along with being healthy, easy, and delicious, this sandwich is also great comfort food. Kids can't get enough of hot tuna and melted cheese, and for adults, your inner child will get happy just thinking about this fun sandwich. Have fun and feel great!

FLAKY FISH QUESADILLA

Quesadillas are such a great choice for a meal filling enough for adults and fun enough for kids. In this recipe, the classic Mexican dish gets a fishy twist with the addition of grilled tilapia. Paired with guacamole, cheese, and perfectly grilled in your air fryer, this quesadilla is as tasty as it is nutritious! *(Recipe serves 1-2 people.)*

INGREDIENTS:

Two 6-inch corn or flour tortilla shells

1 medium sized tilapia fillet, approximately 4 ounces

½ medium sized lemon, sliced

½ an avocado, peeled, pitted and sliced

1 clove of garlic, peeled and finely minced

Pinch of salt and pepper

½ teaspoon of lemon juice

¼ cup of shredded cheddar cheese

¼ cup of shredded mozzarella cheese

INSTRUCTIONS:

1. Preheat the air fryer to 350 degrees.

2. In the oven, grill the tilapia with a little salt and lemon slices in foil on high heat for 20 minutes.

3. Remove fish in foil from the oven, and break the fish meat apart into bite sized pieces with a fork – it should be flaky and chunky when cooked.

4.   While the fish is cooling, combine the avocado, garlic, salt, pepper, and lemon juice in a small mixing bowl; mash lightly, but don't whip. Keep the avocado slightly chunky.

5.   Spread the guacamole on one of the tortillas, then cover with the fish, and then with the cheese. Top with the second tortilla.

6.   Place directly on hot surface of the air frying basket, but be careful not to burn your fingers!

7.   Set air fryer timer for 6 minutes.

8.   After 6 minutes, when the air fryer shuts off, flip the tortillas onto the other side with a spatula; the cheese should be melted enough that it won't fall apart.

9.   Reset air fryer to 350 degrees for another 6 minutes.

10.   After 6 minutes, when the air fryer shuts off, the tortillas should be browned and crisp, and the fish, guacamole and cheese will be hot and delicious inside. Remove with a spatula and let sit on a serving plate to cool for a few minutes before slicing.

NOTES:

A slice of this fishy treat will go great with some salsa and sour cream. Once cooled, the quesadilla is easy to wrap up in foil and enjoy on the go, for a healthy and delicious meal that's as easy as it is filling.

PEPPER CRUSTED FRIED TUNA STEAK

This dinner comes out very fancy looking and gourmet tasting, so no need to tell anyone how easy it is to whip up in the air fryer! This is a wonderful meal to serve for a dinner party or on a date or any time you want to make the best possible impression with a meal that takes things to the next delicious level. *(Recipe serves 3-4 people.)*

INGREDIENTS:

4 medium sized tuna steaks

2 large eggs

3 ounces of melted butter

½ cup of breadcrumbs (Panko, or any other brand or home recipe)

2 tablespoons of ground black pepper

INSTRUCTIONS:

1. Cover the basket of the air fryer with a lining of tin foil, leaving the edges uncovered to allow air to circulate through the basket.

2. Preheat the air fryer to 350 degrees.

3. In a mixing bowl, beat the eggs until fluffy and until the yolks and whites are fully combined. Add the melted butter, and stir thoroughly.

4. In a separate bowl, combine the breadcrumbs and the black pepper.

5. One by one, dunk the tuna steaks into the wet mixture, then roll them in the peppery breadcrumbs, coating completely.

6. Place the coated tuna steaks in the air fryer basket.

7.   Set the air fryer timer for 10 minutes.

8.   When the air fryer shuts off after 10 minutes, the tuna will be partly cooked and the crust beginning to crisp. Using tongs, turn each of the fish steaks over.

9.   Reset the air fryer to 350 degrees for another 10 minutes.

10. After 10 minutes, when the air fryer shuts off, the tuna will be perfectly cooked and the peppery crust will be toasted and crispy. Using tongs, remove from the air fryer and serve.

NOTES:

These tuna steaks go great with a hot vegetable on the side, like creamed spinach or maybe some hot buttery asparagus. They also work great as leftovers in a sandwich – though don't expect to have many leftovers. Everyone will want seconds of this posh gourmet treat!

SWEET AND SAVORY BREADED SHRIMP

This is an awesome recipe for sweet and savory breaded shrimp that will come out fantastic every time in the air fryer. And the best part is that, unlike pretty much any other fried shrimp dish out there, this one doesn't require a lick of added fat or grease, meaning you can savor all the lean protein of the shrimp with that crunchy crust you love, with none of the fat. Enjoy! *(Recipe serves 1-2 people.)*

INGREDIENTS:

½ pound of fresh shrimp, peeled from their shells and rinsed

2 raw eggs

½ cup of breadcrumbs (I like Panko, but any brand or home recipe will do)

½ white onion, peeled and rinsed and finely chopped

½ teaspoon ground ginger

½ teaspoon garlic powder

½ teaspoon of turmeric

½ teaspoon of red chili powder

½ teaspoon of cumin

½ teaspoon of black pepper

½ teaspoon of dry mango powder

Pinch of salt

INSTRUCTIONS:

1. Cover the basket of the air fryer with a lining of tin foil, leaving the edges uncovered to allow air to circulate through the basket.

2. Preheat the air fryer to 350 degrees.

3. In a large mixing bowl, beat the eggs until fluffy and until the yolks and whites are fully combined.

4. Dunk all the shrimp in the egg mixture, fully submerging.

5. In a separate mixing bowl, combine the bread crumbs with all the dry ingredients until evenly blended.

6. One by one, coat the egg covered shrimp in the mixed dry ingredients so that they are fully covered, and place on the foil lined air fryer basket.

7. Set the air fryer timer to 20 minutes.

8. Halfway through the cooking time, shake the handle of the air fryer so that the breaded shrimp jostles inside and fry coverage is even. Or use a spatula to quickly flip them over.

9. After 20 minutes, when the fryer shuts off, the shrimp will be perfectly cooked and their breaded crust golden brown and delicious! Using tongs, remove from the air fryer and set on a serving dish to cool.

NOTES:

A little cocktail or tartar sauce is always great for dipping shrimp, but thanks to the rich seasonings in the breading, these shrimp really don't need anything else to make them absolutely perfect. Serve with salad for some fresh greens, and revel in this crispy, *healthy* air fried goodness!

PISTACHIO CRUSTED LEMON GARLIC SALMON

This is a fantastic dinner for when you want to step it up a notch. This aromatic lemon garlic salmon recipe with a pistachio nut crust is the sort of dish you might expect to find at a gourmet restaurant – except you've prepared it right in your own kitchen, using only the air fryer, and almost none of the added oil or grease that most restaurants would use to create the perfect crispy finish for the fish! *(Recipe serves 3-4 people.)*

INGREDIENTS:

4 medium sized salmon filets

2 raw eggs

3 ounces of melted butter

1 clove of garlic, peeled and finely minced

1 large sized lemon

1 teaspoon of salt

1 tablespoon of parsley, rinsed, patted dry and chopped

1 teaspoon of dill, rinsed, patted dry and chopped

½ cup of pistachio nuts, shelled and coarsely crushed

INSTRUCTIONS:

1. Cover the basket of the air fryer with a lining of tin foil, leaving the edges uncovered to allow air to circulate through the basket.

2. Preheat the air fryer to 350 degrees.

3.   In a mixing bowl, beat the eggs until fluffy and until the yolks and whites are fully combined.

4.   Add the melted butter, the juice of the lemon, the minced garlic, the parsley and the dill to the beaten eggs, and stir thoroughly.

5.   One by one, dunk the salmon filets into the wet mixture, then roll them in the crushed pistachios, coating completely.

6.   Place the coated salmon fillets in the air fryer basket.

7.   Set the air fryer timer for 10 minutes.

8.   When the air fryer shuts off, after 10 minutes, the salmon will be partly cooked and the crust beginning to crisp. Using tongs, turn each of the fish filets over.

9.   Reset the air fryer to 350 degrees for another 10 minutes.

10.   After 10 minutes, when the air fryer shuts off, the salmon will be perfectly cooked and the pistachio crust will be toasted and crispy. Using tongs, remove from the air fryer and serve!

NOTES:

This dinner is sure to impress your family, friends, or even the most hoity toity guests. It's also wonderfully healthy, full of lean protein and omega3 fats – so no need to hold back from second helpings that I know you'll want!

LEMON GARLIC FISH NUGGETS

Everyone will love these little treats – healthy and packed with lean fish protein, perfectly seasoned and lightly breaded, and cooked up all crispy crunchy in the air fryer with no added fat or grease. Best of all, they couldn't be easier to make, which is great, because you'll probably find yourself hankering to whip up a second batch soon. *(Recipe serves 2 people.)*

INGREDIENTS:

Large cod fish filet, approximately 6-8 ounces, fresh or frozen and thawed, cut into bite sized chunks

2 raw eggs

½ cup of breadcrumbs (I like Panko, but any brand or home recipe will do)

1 medium sized lemon

½ tablespoon of garlic powder

Pinch of salt and pepper

INSTRUCTIONS:

1. Cover the basket of the air fryer with a lining of tin foil, leaving the edges uncovered to allow air to circulate through the basket.

2. Preheat the air fryer to 350 degrees.

3. In a large mixing bowl, beat the eggs until fluffy and until the yolks and whites are fully combined. Slice the lemon in half, and squeeze in the juice from one half of the lemon; stir thoroughly. Save the rest of the lemon for serving.

4. Dunk all the fish in the egg and lemon mixture, fully submerging.

5. In a separate mixing bowl, combine the bread crumbs with the garlic powder, and salt and pepper, until evenly mixed.

6. One by one, coat the egg covered fish in the mixed dry ingredients so that they are fully covered, and place on the foil lined air fryer basket.

7. Set the air fryer timer to 20 minutes.

8. Halfway through the cooking time, shake the handle of the air fryer so that the breaded fish jostles inside and fry coverage is even.

9. After 20 minutes, when the fryer shuts off, the fish nuggets will be perfectly cooked and their breaded crust golden brown and delicious! Using tongs, remove from the air fryer and set on a serving dish to cool.

NOTES:

A little tartar sauce is always great for dipping fish, or just squeeze the rest of the lemon on top for a lighter dinner. Serve with a green salad on the side, and enjoy this fresh, *healthy* air fried yumminess!

SPICY COCONUT BREADED SHRIMP

This fantastic dinner offers a taste of the tropics! I love the combination of coconut and chili powder in this light and irresistible breaded coating, and the air fried shrimp are the perfect balance of crispy and succulent. A few bites, and you might imagine yourself on a Caribbean beach without the jetlag! *(Recipe serves 1-2 people.)*

INGREDIENTS:

½ pound of fresh shrimp, peeled from their shells and rinsed

2 raw eggs

½ cup of breadcrumbs (I like Panko, but any brand or home recipe will do)

1 teaspoon of red chili powder

2 tablespoons of dried coconut flakes

Pinch of salt and pepper

INSTRUCTIONS:

1. Cover the basket of the air fryer with a lining of tin foil, leaving the edges uncovered to allow air to circulate through the basket.

2. Preheat the air fryer to 350 degrees.

3. In a large mixing bowl, beat the eggs until fluffy and until the yolks and whites are fully combined.

4. Dunk all the shrimp in the egg mixture, fully submerging.

5. In a separate mixing bowl, combine the bread crumbs, coconut, chili powder, and salt and pepper until evenly blended.

6. One by one, coat the egg covered shrimp in the mixed dry ingredients so that fully covered, and place on the foil lined air fryer basket.

7. Set the air fryer timer to 20 minutes.

8. Halfway through the cooking time, shake the handle of the air fryer so that the breaded shrimp jostles inside and fry coverage is even.

9. After 20 minutes, when the fryer shuts off, the shrimp will be perfectly cooked and their coconut crust will be toasted golden delicious! Using tongs, remove from the air fryer and set on a serving dish to cool.

NOTES:

The flavor of these breaded shrimp is so delicate, I recommend using no dipping sauce at all. Pair with a light salad and maybe some crusty bread and you've got a dinner fit for an island king. Enjoy.

CRISPY CHEESY FISH FINGERS

Frozen fish sticks are cheap and readily available at any grocery store. But why go for second best when you can prepare these awesome cheese encrusted fresh fish fingers so easily, right at home, with zero added fat or grease? This recipe will be a huge hit with the whole family and there's no need to tell them that this dinner is actually very healthy and packed with lean protein. *(Recipe serves 2 people.)*

INGREDIENTS:

Large cod fish filet, approximately 6-8 ounces, fresh or frozen and thawed, cut into 1 ½inch strips

2 raw eggs

½ cup of breadcrumbs (I like Panko, but any brand or home recipe will do)

2 tablespoons of shredded or powdered parmesan cheese

1 tablespoons of shredded cheddar cheese

Pinch of salt and pepper

INSTRUCTIONS:

1. Cover the basket of the air fryer with a lining of tin foil, leaving the edges uncovered to allow air to circulate through the basket.
2. Preheat the air fryer to 350 degrees.
3. In a large mixing bowl, beat the eggs until fluffy and until the yolks and whites are fully combined.
4. Dunk all the fish strips in the beaten eggs, fully submerging.

5. In a separate mixing bowl, combine the bread crumbs with the parmesan, cheddar, and salt and pepper, until evenly mixed.

6. One by one, coat the egg covered fish strips in the mixed dry ingredients so that they're fully covered, and place on the foil lined air fryer basket.

7. Set the air fryer timer to 20 minutes.

8. Halfway through the cooking time, shake the handle of the air fryer so that the breaded fish jostles inside and fry coverage is even.

9. After 20 minutes, when the fryer shuts off, the fish strips will be perfectly cooked and their breaded crust golden brown and delicious! Using tongs, remove from the air fryer and set on a serving dish to cool.

NOTES:

These cheesy fish fingers are so tender and juicy on the inside, and crispy perfect on the outside, they really don't need anything, though a little tartar or ketchup works great as a dipping sauce. Serve with raw carrot sticks or cucumbers to make the entire meal utensil free. Enjoy and have fun!

Vegetarian

Irresistible Veggie Samosas

This classic Indian street food can also be a terrific lunch on the go and believe it or not, you do *not* need to get expensive takeout to enjoy them. Though the genuine articles are usually deep fried in lots of grease, this fantastic air fryer recipe eliminates the need for even a smidge of added oil. So get air frying and relish a little taste of the Asian subcontinent right from your own kitchen! *(Recipe serves 2-3 people.)*

INGREDIENTS:

1 medium to large sized potato, boiled, peeled and diced

¼ cup of green peas, boiled and rinsed

1 teaspoon of garam masala powder

½ teaspoon of ginger garlic paste

½ teaspoon of red chili powder

½ teaspoon of turmeric powder

Pinch of salt and pepper

3 sheets of flaky puff pastry dough (Pillsbury makes an excellent version, or any other brand or home recipe will do fine)

INSTRUCTIONS:

1. Preheat air fryer to 350 degrees.

2. In a mixing bowl, mash the potatoes with a fork or a whisk.

3. Add in the garam masala powder, ginger garlic paste, red chili powder, turmeric powder, and salt and pepper.

4. Add in the peas, and stir entire mixture together until ingredients are evenly blended but be careful not to squish the peas too much! Try to keep most of them whole and plump.

5. Divide the mixture into three equal segments, then form each segment into a ball in your hands. The ingredients should "clump" together easily, though don't worry if they're a bit crumbly.

6. Lay the sheets of puff pastry dough flat on a clean surface.

7. Fill each sheet of dough with one of the three portions of potato pea and spices, then fold the pastry over into a triangle, so it neatly tucks and covers the filling. Seal the edges with a bit of water.

8. Place the three samosas directly in the air fryer basket. Set the air fryer timer to 6 minutes.

9. After 5 minutes, when the fryer shuts off, use tongs to flip the samosas over.

10. Reset the air fryer at 350 degrees for another 6 minutes.

11. After six minutes, when the air fryer shuts off, the samosas will be perfect – hot and spicy on the inside, crispy and flaky and perfectly fried on the outside. Remove with tongs, and set to cool for a few minutes before digging in!

NOTES:

These samosas are wonderful dipped in a little mango chutney or cucumber sauce if you have it, though they're also perfect all on their own. The air fryer keeps the fillings moist and delicious on the inside, so even if you have to save them for later and eat them cold, you know they'll be an exotic and spicy lunchtime treat!

WORLD'S GREATEST GRILLED CHEESE

Everyone knows what makes a perfect grilled cheese sandwich: bread, cheese, and tons of butter in the frying pan, plus a little more butter for good measure, and then some butter on top of that. It's delicious, but it's not exactly the healthiest meal in the world. The air fried version below, however, delivers all the crispy, gooey, fried cheesy goodness with almost no butter at all. So, no – this is not your grandmother's grilled cheese sandwich. It's just as delicious, but a lot healthier! *(Recipe serves 1-2 people.)*

INGREDIENTS:

4 slices of white bread

2 slices of premium cheddar cheese

2 slices of provolone cheese

2 slices of Swiss cheese

1 small pat of butter

INSTRUCTIONS:

1. Preheat the air fryer to 360 degrees.

2. Lightly spread the butter on both sides of each slice of bread – and I do mean lightly! You don't need more than a very thin coat on each side.

3. Lay the slices of bread on the air frying basket, side by side. They should fit snuggly, with the edges barely touching (it's fine if they do, as long as they don't overlap).

4. Set the air fryer timer to 6 minutes.

5. After 6 minutes, when the air fryer shuts off, the bread should be beginning to crisp and brown. Using a spatula, flip over each slice of bread.

6. Cover two of the bread slices with a layer of cheddar cheese, and the other two slices with a layer of the provolone and then the Swiss cheese.

7. Set the air fryer to 320 degrees for 10 minutes.

8. After 10 minutes, when the air fryer shuts off, the cheeses should be melted and lightly bubbling, and the bread should be perfectly toasted to a golden brown.

9. Using a spatula, place the cheddar covered bread slices on a serving plate, and top each with the provolone and Swiss covered slices.

10. Slice in half once cool enough to handle, and serve with a side of soup, salad, or – most likely – a second helping!

NOTES:

If you have to wrap up this sandwich to go, make sure you wait until the cheese is cool enough that it won't stick to the tin foil. And don't worry, this sandwich tastes just as good cold as it does warm – and because there's so little butter, the bread will stay crisp and toasted, and won't get soggy. This is, indeed, the world's greatest grilled cheese.

BLACK AND WHITE VEGETARIAN PIZZA

In your humble author's opinion, there are few more delicious pizza topping combinations than browned white onions and sliced black olives. Combined with silky smooth tomato laced ricotta and topped with just enough mozzarella to keep things gooey and delicious, this pizza is absolutely irresistible and with so little added grease, it can be enjoyed guiltfree! *(Recipe serves 1-2 people.)*

INGREDIENTS:

1 pre-prepared 6-inch pizza pie crust (Mama Mary and Patty's Gourmet Pizza both make great versions, or feel free to use the brand of your choice or a homemade preparation), defrosted if necessary.

¼ cup of fresh ricotta cheese

½ tablespoon of tomato paste or pureed tomato concentrate

½ a medium sized raw white onion, sliced and coarsely chopped

¼ cup of black olives, pitted and sliced

¼ cup of shredded or grated mozzarella cheese

INSTRUCTIONS:

1. Preheat the air fryer to 350 degrees.

2. In a small bowl, combine the ricotta and tomato paste until evenly blended; the mixture should be a rosy pink color, though feel free to add more or less tomato depending on personal preference. Set aside.

3. Lay the pizza dough flat on a sheet of parchment paper or tin foil, cut just large enough to hold the entire pie crust.

4. Using a fork, stab the pizza dough several times across the surface – piercing the pie crust will allow air to circulate throughout the crust and ensure even cooking.

5. With a deep soup spoon, ladle the ricotta and tomato mixture onto the pizza dough, and spread evenly in expanding circles over the surface of the piecrust. Be sure to leave at least ½ inch of bare dough around the edges, to ensure that extra crispy crunchy bite of the crust!

6. Distribute the onions and olives evenly over the sauce covered dough, then sprinkle the grated cheese in an even layer on top.

7. Set the air fryer timer to 1-2 minutes, and place the pizza with foil or paper on the fryer's basket surface. Again, be sure to leave the edges of the basket uncovered to allow for proper air circulation, and don't let your bare fingers touch the hot surface!

8. After 1-2 minutes, when the air fryer shuts off, the cheese should be perfectly melted and lightly crisped, and the pie crust should be golden brown.

9. Using a spatula – or two, if necessary! – remove the pizza from the air fryer basket and set on a serving plate. Wait a few minutes until the pie is cool enough to handle, then cut into slices, serve and enjoy!

NOTES:

Feel free to adjust the cooking time depending on personal preference – an extra minute or two will get an extra crispy crust, and a minute or two less will ensure a fluffier, doughier consistency. However you cook it, this filling vegetarian dish is an absolute winner. While it should be enough to satisfy two people, I'm betting you'll love it so much you'll want go for that second helping and gobble it up by yourself. And with such nutritious ingredients and no unnecessary fat, why not indulge?

LOVELY LENTIL QUESADILLA

Lentils are so nutritious, perhaps that's why they have an unearned reputation of being boring. This awesome quesadilla recipe turns that reputation on its head, with zesty peppers and onions, spicy pepper jack cheese, and a crunchy air fried all around crust. Believe it or not, it's time to get excited about lentils! *(Recipe serves 1-2 people.)*

INGREDIENTS:

Two 6-inch corn or flour tortilla shells

½ cup of cooked lentils, rinsed and drained

½ medium sized white onion, sliced

½ medium sized red pepper, sliced

½ medium sized green pepper, sliced

½ medium sized yellow pepper, sliced

½ cup of shredded pepper jack cheese

INSTRUCTIONS:

1. Preheat the air fryer to 320 degrees.

2. In the oven on high heat for 20 minutes, grill the lentils, onion and peppers in foil in the same pan, allowing the moisture from the vegetables and the juice from the lentils to mingle together.

3. Remove the lentils and vegetables in foil from the oven. While they're cooling, sprinkle half the shredded cheese over one of the tortillas, then cover with the lentils, onions, and peppers, and then layer on the rest of the shredded cheese. Top with the second tortilla.

4. Place directly on the hot surface of the air frying basket, but be careful not to burn your fingers!

5. Set air fryer timer for 3 minutes.

6. After 2 minutes, when the air fryer shuts off, flip the tortillas on-to the other side with a spatula; the cheese should be melted enough that it won't fall apart, but be careful anyway not to spill any toppings!

7. Reset air fryer to 320 degrees for another 3 minutes.

8. After 3 minutes, when the air fryer shuts off, the tortillas should be browned and perfect, and the lentils, onion, peppers and cheese will be crispy and hot and delicious. Remove with tongs and let sit on a serving plate to cool for a few minutes before slic-ing.

NOTES:

This quesadilla is so delicious; you'll barely remember that it's also ex-tremely healthy. Lentils are an excellent source of protein without any animal fat, so if you feel yourself energized for the rest of the day, don't be surprised – just enjoy it!

BLACK BEAN AND CHEESE VEGGIE BURGER

This is such a perfect recipe when you want a lean, protein packed dinner that everyone will love. These black bean and cheddar veggie burgers are so tasty, vegetarians and meat eaters alike will gobble them down. Thanks to the air fryer, no one needs to feel guilty for the seconds they will definitely want. *(Recipe serves 2 people.)*

INGREDIENTS:

1 cup of black beans, cooked or canned, rinsed and drained

½ cup of shredded cheddar cheese

1 raw egg

Pinch of salt and pepper

1 cup of bread crumbs (Panko works great, but so would any other brand or homemade recipe)

INSTRUCTIONS:

1. Cover the basket of the air fryer with a lining of tin foil, leaving the edges uncovered to allow air to circulate through the basket.

2. Preheat the air fryer to 350 degrees.

3. In a mixing bowl, beat the egg until fluffy and until the yolk and white are fully combined.

4. In a separate bowl, mash the beans with a fork. It's okay to still have a little texture with the beans. Mix in the cheese, salt and pepper and mix until evenly combined. Continuing to mash and stir, add in approximately half the bread crumbs. Last, add the egg to the bean mixture.

5. When the combination is evenly mixed, it should be thick enough to shape into patties with your hands. Divide the mixture evenly and shape, adding more bread crumbs to firm up if necessary.

6. Coat each patty in the remaining bread crumbs so that they are fully covered, then place on the foil covered air fryer basket. (Careful, because the device will be hot!)

7. Set the air fryer timer for 15 minutes.

8. After 15 minutes, the air fryer will turn off and the breaded coating on the patties should be starting to brown.

9. Using tongs – careful not to burn your fingers! – turn each veggie patty over to ensure a full allover fry.

10. Reset the air fryer to 320 degrees for 10 minutes.

11. After 10 minutes, when the air fryer shuts off, remove the veggie burgers using tongs and set on a serving plate, with or without buns.

NOTES:

One of the best things about these veggie burgers is how versatile they are. They work great as a "regular" burger with some cheese and ketchup on a bun, or else can be crumbled and served with rice or pasta. There's really no wrong way to eat these veggie burgers. They're always a delicious dinner!

LEAN LENTIL PATTY

Without red meat, there are few ways to give your body a full dose of iron rich nutrients, unless you've got lentils on hand. This dish should be a weekly staple for vegetarians who want to maintain a healthy iron content – and for anyone else who's keen on getting nutrient rich protein without overdosing on beef. As tasty as they are healthy, these lentil patties are absolute winners. *(Recipe serves 2-3 people.)*

INGREDIENTS:

1 cup of black or brown lentils, cooked or canned, rinsed and drained

½ cup of grated American cheese

2 raw eggs

Pinch of salt and pepper

1 cup of bread crumbs (Panko works great, but so would any other brand or homemade recipe)

INSTRUCTIONS:

1. Cover the basket of the air fryer with a lining of tin foil, leaving the edges uncovered to allow air to circulate through the basket.

2. Preheat the air fryer to 350 degrees.

3. In a mixing bowl, beat the eggs until fluffy and until the yolks and whites are fully combined.

4. Add in the lentils and cheese, and mash into the eggs until evenly combined. Continuing to mash and stir, add in approximately half the bread crumbs, and salt and pepper to taste.

5. When the combination is evenly mixed, it should be thick enough to shape into 2 patties with your hands. Divide the mixture evenly and shape, adding more bread crumbs to firm up if necessary.

6. Coat each patty in the remaining bread crumbs so that they are fully covered, then place on the foil covered air fryer basket. (Careful, because the device will be hot!)

7. Set the air fryer timer for 15 minutes.

8. After 15 minutes, the air fryer will turn off and the breaded coating on the patties should be starting to brown.

9. Using tongs – careful not to burn your fingers! – turn each lentil patty over to ensure a full allover fry.

10. Reset the air fryer to 320 degrees for 10 minutes.

11. After 10 minutes, when the air fryer shuts off, remove the lentil patties using tongs and set on a serving plate, with or without buns.

NOTES:

These patties go great on a bun with some lettuce, tomato, and ketchup, or else they're the ideal topper to a fresh green salad. Really, nothing beats the power punch of cheesy lentil patties, both for your health, and your taste buds. Treat both right as you enjoy this hearty, wholesome dinner.

PASTAS AND SIDE DISHES

PASTA

CHEESY SPINACH STUFFED SHELLS

Everyone will be begging for a helping once they smell the cheesy, creamy goodness of spinach stuffed shells crisped in the air fryer. This is a perfect comfort food dinner for cold nights when you want something warm and soothing at the end of a day, and it's also a great dose of vegetables that kids will love. *(Recipe serves 3-4 people.)*

INGREDIENTS:

4 jumbo pasta shells, cooked in boiling water and drained

1 cup of ricotta cheese

1 cup of shredded mozzarella cheese

1 cup of spinach, cooked, rinsed and chopped

1 medium sized egg

1 cup of marinara sauce (store-bought or homemade; any recipe will do)

INSTRUCTIONS:

1. Preheat the air fryer to 360 degrees.
2. In a mixing bowl, beat the egg until fluffy and until the yolk and white are fully combined.
3. Mix in the ricotta, mozzarella, and the chopped spinach, until all the ingredients are evenly combine.
4. One by one, stuff the mixture into each of the cooked pasta shells.

5.   In a 6-inch heat safe pan, spread half the marinara sauce, then place the stuffed shells on the sauce covered pan, with the seams facing up. Spread the rest of the marinara sauce over the tops.

6.   Place the pan inside the air fryer basket (carefully, because it will be hot!), and set the air fryer timer to 25 minutes.

7.   After 25 minutes, when the fryer shuts off, the stuffed shells will be wonderfully cooked, crispy on the outside but still moist from the marinara sauce, with the spinach and cheeses inside gooey and delicious. Remove from the air fryer basket using a spatula, and serve while hot.

NOTES:

These stuffed shells are such a treat – eating them is like getting a big hug from your very own Italian Mamma. And thanks to the air fryer and no need for additional butter or grease to get that awesome crust around the shells, you really can feel good about eating this.

VEGGIE DELIGHT FRIED STUFFED CANNELLONI

This dinner packs a nutrient rich punch, and tastes simply decadent. That's a difficult balance to achieve, though less so with the air fryer keeping added grease and fat to a minimum. The best part about this recipe is how it "hides" veggies in all that cheesy goodness, a terrific way to get kids to eat their vegetables with a smile! *(Recipe serves 3-4 people.)*

INGREDIENTS:

4 cannelloni pasta shells, cooked in boiling water and drained

1 cup of ricotta cheese

1 cup of shredded mozzarella cheese

1/2 cup of broccoli, cooked, rinsed, and finely chopped

1/2 cup of spinach, cooked, rinsed and chopped

1 medium sized egg

1 cup of marinara sauce (store-bought or homemade; any recipe will do)

INSTRUCTIONS:

1. Preheat the air fryer to 360 degrees.

2. In a mixing bowl, beat the egg until fluffy and until the yolk and white are fully combined.

3. Mix into the egg the ricotta, mozzarella, and the chopped broccoli, until all the ingredients are evenly combine.

4. One by one, stuff the mixture into each of the cooked cannelloni pasta shells.

5. In a 6-inch heat safe pan, spread half the marinara sauce, then place the stuffed cannelloni shells on the sauce covered pan. Spread the rest of the marinara sauce over the tops.

6. Place the pan inside the air fryer basket (carefully, because it will be hot!), and set the air fryer timer to 25 minutes.

7. After 25 minutes, when the fryer shuts off, the stuffed cannelloni shells will be wonderfully cooked, crispy on the outside but still moist from the marinara sauce, with the broccoli and cheeses inside gooey and delicious. Remove from the air fryer basket using a spatula, and serve while hot.

NOTES:

These stuffed cannelloni are so filling, so warming, and perfectly healthy. They're a complete and balanced meal all on their own, and while they taste best when hot, they're also delectable after a few hours in the fridge if you have any leftovers. Eat up and eat well!

ULTIMATE EGGPLANT PARMESAN

I love a good eggplant parmesan – the classic Italian vegetarian dish that's as healthy as it is delectable. This recipe gets it just right, with a perfect savory crust and the ideal ratio of cheese to sauce. It's so good, it's hard to believe that it's made with healthy ingredients, and better yet, this dish couldn't be easier to prepare! *(Recipe serves 1-2 people.)*

INGREDIENTS:

4 thick cut slices of eggplant

1 cup of breadcrumbs (Panko brand works well)

2 medium sized eggs

Pinch of salt and pepper

1 tablespoon of dried oregano

1 cup of marinara sauce (store-bought or homemade will do equally well)

2 slices of provolone cheese

1 tablespoon of parmesan cheese

INSTRUCTIONS:

1. Cover the basket of the air fryer with a lining of tin foil, leaving the edges uncovered to allow air to circulate through the basket.

2. Preheat the air fryer to 350 degrees.

3. In a mixing bowl, beat the eggs until fluffy and until the yolks and whites are fully combined, and set aside.

4. In a separate mixing bowl, combine the breadcrumbs, oregano, salt and pepper, and set aside.

5.   One by one, dip the raw eggplant slices into the bowl with dry ingredients, coating both sides. Then submerge into the bowl with wet ingredients, then dip again into the dry ingredients. This double coating will ensure an extra crisp and delicious air fry!

6.   Lay the coated eggplant on the foil covering the air fryer basket, in a single flat layer.

7.   Set the air fryer timer for 10 minutes.

8.   After 10 minutes, the air fryer will turn off and the eggplant should be midway cooked and the breaded coating starting to brown.

9.   Using tongs – careful not to burn your fingers! – turn each piece of eggplant over to ensure a full allover fry.

10.   Reset the air fryer to 320 degrees for another 7 minutes.

11.   While the eggplant is cooking, pour half the marinara sauce into a 6-inch heat safe pan.

12.   After 7 minutes, when the air fryer shuts off, remove the fried eggplant using tongs and set in the marinara covered pan. Drizzle the rest of the marinara sauce over the fried eggplant, then place the slices of provolone cheese atop both of them and sprinkle the parmesan cheese over the entire pan.

13.   Reset the air fryer to 350 degrees for 5 minutes.

14.   After 5 minutes, when the air fryer shuts off, remove the dish from the air fryer using tongs or oven mitts. The eggplant will be perfectly crisped and the cheese melted and lightly toasted. Serve while hot over boiled pasta!

NOTES:

This dish obviates the need to choose between a healthy dinner and a delicious dinner. So sit back, relax, and end your day with this meal that offers both in one perfect, crispy, cheese covered classic. Now that's what I call *delizioso!*

AIR FRIED RAVIOLI

Whether you use this as an appetizer or a quick, simple meal both kids and adults will love these crunchy raviolis. The air fryer insures that the outside has that perfect crisp texture, yet the middle stays cheesy and gooey. These raviolis come together quickly and while they are "frying" in your air fryer you can pull together the rest of the meal. Quick, easy and delicious is my favorite combination! (Serves 3-4 people.)

INGREDIENTS:

1-2 premade frozen ravioli

2 eggs

2 cups flour

2 cups of breadcrumbs (Panko brand works well.)

pinch of salt and pepper

INSTRUCTIONS:

1. Cover the basket of the air fryer with a lining of tin foil, leaving the edges uncovered to allow air to circulate through the basket.

2. Preheat the air fryer to 375 degrees.

3. In a mixing bowl, beat the eggs until fluffy and until the yolks and whites are fully combined, and set aside.

4. Add a pinch of salt and pepper to the flour and mix to combine. Place flour in a shallow bowl. Place breadcrumbs in a separate shallow bowl.

5.   Using all three bowls the eggs, the flour and the bread-
        crumbs alternate dipping each ravioli into them to coat.
        Start with eggs, then dredge in the flour. Dip again in the
        egg mixture and finally coat with breadcrumbs. Place on the
        basket of the air fryer.

6.   Repeat with remaining raviolis. You made need to work in
        batches if the air fryer basket gets full.

7.   Set the timer for 20 minutes. After 20 minutes, when air
        fryer shuts off, carefully remove the raviolis from the bas-
        ket. Prepare and cook the next batch. Enjoy while warm
        with marinara.

NOTES:

These raviolis should be perfectly cooked and super cheesy in the middle. Serving with warm marinara sauce completes the true Italian feeling, plus it's just fun! Experiment with your favorite filling in the frozen
raviolis. My favorite is a cheese and spinach mixture!

MACARONI AND CHEESE

The air fryer puts the perfect cheesy "crust" on this delicious macaroni and cheese dish. Our family can't help it, it's our favorite part! After you try this easy recipe for homemade macaroni and cheese, you'll never want to fool with boxed macaroni again. (Serves 3-4.)

INGREDIENTS:

4 cups cooked elbow

2 cups grated cheddar cheese

3 egg, beaten

1/2 cup sour cream

4 tablespoons of butter

1/2 teaspoon of salt

1 cup milk

INSTRUCTIONS:

1. Preheat the air fryer to 350 degrees.

2. Boil and drain the macaroni. While it is still hot, add 1 1/2 cups of cheese and the butter and allow them to melt.

3. Combine the beaten eggs, milk, sour cream and salt. Stir them into the macaroni and mix gently.

4. Pour the macaroni and cheese into a deep 6-inch ceramic heat safe dish that has been lightly sprayed with nonstick cooking spray.

5. Place the dish into the basket of the air fryer and set the timer for 20 minutes.

6. After 20 minutes, when the air fryer shuts off, sprinkle the remaining 1/2 cup of grated cheese onto the top of the macaroni.

7. Set the timer for 510 minutes, depending on how well done you prefer your cheesy crust.

8. When cooking is complete, remove from the air fryer using oven mitts or tongs, and set on a heat safe surface to cool for a few minutes before cutting.

NOTES:

Kids will really love this yummy treat and you can feel good because you know exactly what is in each bite. And I won't lie, I crave this cheesy dish just as much as the kids. Cooking it in the air fryer just makes it easy for the times when its too hot to turn on the oven, or any other time you want a home cooked dish but an oven is just not available.

VEGGIES AND SIDE DISHES

CAULIFLOWER AND CHEESE TART

The classic cauliflower and cheese comfort dish gets a crunchy, delicious makeover in this awesome recipe for a savory, crunchy tart. This dish is an outstanding side dish for a special occasion and will be sure to leave your guests satisfied. *(Recipe serves 3-4 people.)*

INGREDIENTS:

Premade savory crust, chilled and rolled flat to make a 6-inch pie crust (Pillsbury and Marie Callender's both offer great options, or feel free to use any other brand or homemade recipe).

2 eggs

¼ cup of milk

Pinch of salt and pepper

½ cup of cooked cauliflower, finely chopped

¼ cup of shredded mozzarella cheese

¼ cup of shredded cheddar cheese

INSTRUCTIONS:

1. Preheat the air fryer to 360 degrees.

2. Press the premade crust into a 6-inch pie tin, or any appropriately sized glass or ceramic heat safe dish. Press and trim at the edges if necessary.

3. With a fork, pierce several holes in the dough to allow air circulation and prevent cracking of the crust while cooking.

4. In a mixing bowl, beat the eggs until fluffy and until the yolks and white are evenly combined.

5. Add milk, cauliflower, salt and pepper, and half the cheddar and mozzarella cheese to the eggs.

6. Set the rest of the cheese aside for now, and stir the mixture until completely blended.

7. Pour the mixture into the pie crust, slowly and carefully to avoid splashing. The mixture should almost fill the crust, but not completely – leaving a ¼ inch of crust at the edges.

8. Set the air fryer timer for 15 minutes.

9. After 15 minutes, the air fryer will shut off, and the tart will already be firm and the crust beginning to brown. Sprinkle the rest of the cheddar and mozzarella cheese on top of the tart filling.

10. Reset the air fryer at 360 degrees for 5 minutes.

11. After 5 minutes, when the air fryer shuts off, the cheese will have formed an exquisite crust on top and the tart will be golden brown and perfect. Remove from the air fryer using oven mitts or tongs, and set on a heat safe surface to cool.

NOTES:

Everyone will be pleading for a taste of this homey yet elevated dish – the perfect variation on the traditional old classic. Go on and share if you like – though don't forget to leave enough for a second helping for yourself. Trust me, you'll want it.

BLACK BEAN AND POTATO FRITTATA

Enjoy a taste of Spain with this delicious protein packed side dish. Serve a small slice with your dinner, or fix a side salad and make it a meal! It's as easy to prepare as it is delectable to eat. *(Recipe serves 4-6 people.)*

INGREDIENTS:

½ cup of black beans, cooked, rinsed and drained

1 large potato, or two medium sized potatoes, washed, boiled and sliced

3 raw eggs

Pinch of salt and pepper

1 small pat of butter or margarine

½ cup of shredded cheddar cheese

INSTRUCTIONS:

1. Preheat the air fryer to 350 degrees.

2. Lightly grease a 6-inch heat safe pan or baking dish

3. In a mixing bowl, beat the eggs until fluffy and until the whites and yolks are combined.

4. Stir in the beans, half the cheese, salt and pepper, making sure that the cheese doesn't clump together and all the ingredients are evenly spread.

5. Pour the entire mixture into the greased baking dish.

6. Place the potato slices inside the baking dish, evenly spacing among the bean and egg mixture.

7. Set the baking dish in the air fryer basket – careful not to burn your fingers! – and set the air fryer timer for 15 minutes.

8. After 15 minutes, when the air fryer shuts off, sprinkle the rest of the shredded cheddar over the dish.

9. Set the air fryer to 330 degrees for 10 minutes.

10. After 10 minutes, when the air fryer shuts off, remove the baking dish using oven mitts. Turn the dish upside down over a serving plate, and the frittata should slip out easily, with a perfect cheesy crust. Enjoy hot or cold!

NOTES:

This is such a versatile dish it fits into too many categories to choose just one. Dinner, side dish, even for breakfast this dish is sure to be a hit!

SUMMER VEGETABLE MEDLEY

Using the air fryer to prepare vegetables is a no brainer, especially in the summer when it is just too hot to turn on the oven. The vegetables remain crispy on the outside but soft when you bite into them. Your family and friends will be begging you to bring this summer vegetable medley to the next barbecue! (Serves 4 6 people.)

INGREDIENTS:

1/2 pound of carrots, cut into 1 inch chunks

1 pound zucchini, cut in half lengthwise and sliced into 3/4 inch pieces

1 pound yellow squash, cut in half lengthwise and sliced into 3/4 inch pieces

6 teaspoons of olive oil, divided

1 teaspoon salt

1/2 teaspoon pepper

1/2 teaspoon garlic powder

2-3 tablespoons Parmesan cheese

INSTRUCTIONS:

1. Cover the basket of the air fryer with a lining of tin foil, leaving the edges uncovered to allow air to circulate through the basket.

2. Preheat the air fryer to 390 degrees.

3. In a bowl, toss the carrots and 2 teaspoons of olive oil until carrots are well coated.

4. Add the carrots to the air fryer basket and set timer for 5 minutes.

5. While the carrots are cooking, mix the squash and zucchini together and drizzle the remaining 4 teaspoon. olive oil on top. Mix well to coat, then season with salt, pepper and garlic powder.

6. When the carrots are done, add the zucchini and squash mixture to the basket of the air fryer and set timer for 30 minutes. Mix the vegetables several times during cooking to ensure they are cooked evenly.

7. After 30 minutes, when the air fryer shuts off, the vegetables should be nice and tender. Remove from the basket and top with 2-3 tablespoons of Parmesan cheese.

NOTES:

This recipe is the perfect way to use the variety of vegetables that come from your garden or farmer's market. The light seasonings really let the vegetable flavors be the star of the show. Experiment with all the different vegetables in your garden and find your favorite mixture!

CHEESY TRUFFLE POTATO CROQUETTES

This delectable snack is a perfect side dish to any dinner, but you'll find yourself craving them in between meals as well. The truffle oil hits the perfect balance with the crispy browned potato, and their light crispy coating makes them positively irresistible. As an appetizer or side dish, these croquettes are for you! *(Recipe serves 3-4 people.)*

2 large potatoes, peeled, boiled and cubed

2 raw eggs

2 tablespoons of melted butter

1 tablespoon of truffle oil

½ tablespoon of flour

Pinch of salt and pepper

INSTRUCTIONS:

1. Preheat the air fryer to 350 degrees.

2. Line the inside of your air fryer basket with tin foil, leaving enough space around the edges for air to circulate through the basket.

3. In a small mixing bowl, beat the eggs until fluffy and until the yolks and whites are combined. Set aside.

4. In another small mixing bowl, combine the flour, salt and pepper

5. In a larger, third mixing bowl, combine the potatoes, butter, and truffle oil, mixing until all the ingredients are fully combined and the potatoes are mashed (lumps are fine).

6. Divide the potato mixture into even portions and shape into small bite sized patties. They should make between 6-8, depending on the size of the potatoes used.

7. One by one, dunk each potato patty into the bowl with the beaten eggs, coating thoroughly, then roll in the dry flour, salt and pepper mixture to cover all sides.

8. Place each coated potato patty into the foil lined air fryer basket, side by side but not overlapping. They should fit snugly on the surface of the air fryer basket.

9. Set the air fryer timer to 20 minutes. Halfway through cooking, shake the handle of the air fryer basket to jostle the croquettes and ensure a nice even crisp fry.

10. After 20 minutes, when the air fryer shuts off, the croquettes will be perfect – crispy and golden on the outside, with the truffle laced potatoes fragrant and delicious on the inside. Serve while hot.

NOTES:

These are an amazing treat with any dish, and delectable enough to eat on their own. They don't hold up as well once they're cold, but they never last long enough to get cold anyway. Everyone will gobble these up while they're still hot and fresh, so thank goodness it's easy and fast to whip up a new batch!

SWEET AND SPICY FRIED OKRA BITES

The okra plant is a wonder of nature and so delicious when lightly battered and crispy fried. This delicious appetizer or side dish packs a ton of nutrients in its green seed pods, including rich doses of Vitamin C, folate and magnesium. This recipe is also an ideal standalone snack when you want something that's truly healthy and 100% yummy. *(Recipe serves 2-3 people.)*

INGREDIENTS:

1 cup of fresh okra, rinsed and sliced into bite sized pieces

1 cup of breadcrumbs (Panko brand works well)

2 medium sized eggs

Pinch of ground black pepper

1 teaspoon of hot chili flakes

2 teaspoons of hot sauce

INSTRUCTIONS:

1. Cover the basket of the air fryer with a lining of tin foil, leaving the edges uncovered to allow air to circulate through the basket.

2. Preheat the air fryer to 350 degrees.

3. In a mixing bowl, beat the eggs until fluffy and until the yolks and whites are fully combined. Add in the hot sauce, stir thoroughly, and set aside.

4. In a separate mixing bowl, combine the breadcrumbs, chili flakes, and pepper, and set aside.

5. One by one, dip each piece of okra into the bowl with dry ingredients, coating all sides; then submerge into the bowl with wet ingredients, then dip again into the dry ingredients. This double coating will ensure an extra crisp and delicious air fry!

6. Lay the coated okra pieces on the foil covering the air fryer basket, in a single flat layer.

7. Set the air fryer timer for 15 minutes.

8. Shake the handle of the air fryer basket several times during cooking, to jostle the okra and ensure a good even fry.

9. After 15 minutes, the okra should be crispy, golden brown and perfect. Serve and enjoy while they're hot!

NOTES:

Thanks to the wondrous okra maintaining their firm juicy crunch so very well, these nibbles don't need any sort of dipping sauce, though for those who really want one, cucumber sauce or ranch is great.

GARLIC SEASONED BAKED POTATOES

Potatoes are a heart friendly food due to being high in fiber and lacking in cholesterol. They are also delicious! By preparing them in the air fryer the skin of the potato becomes crisp while the inside is hot and fluffy. These potatoes are easy to prepare and will become a beloved staple in your dinner routine. (Serves 3 people.)

INGREDIENTS:

3 small baking potatoes
1-2 tablespoons olive oil

1 tablespoon salt

1 tablespoon minced garlic

1 teaspoon parsley, finely chopped

INSTRUCTIONS:

1. Cover the basket of the air fryer with a lining of tin foil, leaving the edges uncovered to allow air to circulate through the basket.

2. Preheat the air fryer to 392 degrees.

3. Scrub the potatoes in warm water. Use a fork to pierce several holes in the potatoes to allow steam to vent.

4. Rub the olive oil all over the skins of the potatoes. Roll the potatoes in the minced garlic and parsley, using your fingers to help it stick if necessary. Finally, sprinkle liberally with salt.

5. Add the potatoes into the basket of the air fryer and set the timer for 40 minutes.

6. When the air fryer shuts off, test the potatoes with a fork to make sure they are tender. If they need more time, reset the timer in 5 minute intervals.

7. Using tongs – careful not to burn your fingers! – remove the potatoes from the basket and serve along with your favorite toppings.

NOTES:

Potatoes make not only a delicious side dish, but paired with the right toppings, they can make a meal all by themselves. Of course, the standard toppings, such as butter, sour cream and cheese are all great, but to really jazz up your potato try a little salsa, broccoli, or even chili.

CRUNCHY CRISPY KALE CHIPS

Forget all the punchlines about hipsters and kale chips, this simple, nutritious snack is just too delicious to dismiss. Kale chips couldn't be easier to prepare with the air fryer, and they make the perfect go to snack when you just need something to munch on while working or studying. Eat up, and rest easy knowing you're doing your body good! *(Recipe serves 2-3 people.)*

INGREDIENTS:

6 ounces of fresh kale leaves, thoroughly rinsed, shredded and patted dry
2 teaspoons of olive oil
Pinch of salt and pepper

INSTRUCTIONS:

1. Cover the basket of the air fryer with a lining of tin foil, leaving the edges uncovered to allow air to circulate through the basket.

2. Preheat the air fryer to 320 degrees.

3. In a bowl, toss the kale with the olive oil, salt and pepper.

4. Arrange the kale on the lined air fryer basket. The leaves will overlap a few layers, which is just fine – thanks to the oil they won't stick, and they're light enough to allow full air circulation during cooking.

5. Set the air fryer timer to 10 minutes. Throughout the duration, vigorously shake the handle of the air fryer several times to jostle the kale leaves and ensure a good even fry.

6. After 10 minutes, when the air fryer shuts off, the kale will be perfectly cooked, crispy and crunchy and seasoned just right. Serve hot or cold!

NOTES:

This is the kind of snack you can keep around all day long. Munch through multiple batches if you like (I do!). If you're anything like me, you won't get sick of them and your body will thank you! There's a reason kale chips have become so popular lately. It's because they're delicious, as well as being totally healthy. Enjoy!

POTATOES AU GRATIN

This classic French side dish comes out perfectly with this air fried recipe. The potatoes and cheese are crisp and delicious on the outside, and hot and gooey on the inside. This is the perfect side to serve with any meat dish for dinner, and by itself it's the ultimate comfort food snack. *(Recipe serves 3-4 people.)*

INGREDIENTS:

2 large or 3 medium sized potatoes, peeled and sliced

½ cup of milk

½ cup of sour cream

Pinch of salt and pepper

1 teaspoon of ground nutmeg

½ cup of grated Gruyere cheese

INSTRUCTIONS:

1. Cover the basket of the air fryer with a lining of tin foil, leaving the edges uncovered to allow air to circulate through the basket.

2. Preheat the air fryer to 350 degrees.

3. In a mixing bowl, combine the milk, sour cream, salt, pepper, and nutmeg. Mix well.

4. Coat each potato slice in the wet mixture, then arrange on a heat safe 6-inch metal or ceramic baking dish. Pour the rest of the wet mixture into the baking dish, covering the potatoes.

5. Sprinkle the grated cheese over the top of the entire mixture, and set the baking dish in the air fryer.

6.   Set the air fryer timer to 20 minutes.

7.   After 20 minutes, when the air fryer shuts off, remove the baking dish using oven mitts and serve while warm.

NOTES:

This dish comes out perfect every time, and simply couldn't be yummier. I'm not sure what it is about hot creamy potatoes covered in crispy, gooey cheese that gets me so happy. I just know that I always want a second helping!

HONEY GLAZED CARROTS

I've found people either loves carrots, or they loathe them. My husband was firmly in the loathing camp until he tried this recipe for honey carrots. Suddenly he can't get enough of them. The air fryer is a wonderful tool for roasting this vegetable as it makes them slightly crisp on the outside, while still being tender. The honey roasts with the carrots adding delightful flavor that will have your family asking for more! (Serves 4 people.)

INGREDIENTS:

3 cups of carrots, either baby carrots or carrots that have been cut into 1-2 inch chunks

1 tablespoon olive oil

1 tablespoon honey, plus 1 teaspoon for drizzling

Pinch of salt and pepper

INSTRUCTIONS:

1. Cover the basket of the air fryer with a lining of tin foil, leaving the edges uncovered to allow air to circulate through the basket.

2. Preheat the air fryer to 390 degrees.

3. Combine the carrots with the olive oil and honey. Toss to make sure carrots are well coated.

4. Add desired amount of salt and pepper.

5. Dump the carrot mixture into the basket of the air fryer. Set the air fryer timer for 20 minutes.

6.   After 20 minutes, when the air fryer shuts off, remove the carrot mixture from the basket. Drizzle 1 teaspoon of honey over the top, serve hot and enjoy!

NOTES:

The olive oil and the honey in this recipe really work together magically to make these carrots quite tasty. Be sure to add a little salt which counterbalances the sweetness nicely. Also, don't feel shy about drizzling just a little extra honey over the top right after you pull them from the air fryer basket.

THE ULTIMATE BAY SEASONED FRENCH FRIES

Fun fact: The beloved deep fried potato was first eaten in the Dutch speaking part of modern day Belgium. I'm not sure how France managed to get this timeless treat credited to their culture, but we can save that history lesson for another day. Everybody loves a good fry, and this version with bay seasoning is simply perfection. (Recipe serves 2-3 people)

INGREDIENTS:

2 large or 3 medium sized potatoes, washed, peeled, and sliced into strips or fries approximately ½inch thick

3 cups of water

2 teaspoons of olive oil

½ teaspoon of Old Bay seasoning

Pinch of salt and pepper

INSTRUCTIONS:

1. Cover the basket of the air fryer with a lining of tin foil, leaving the edges uncovered to allow air to circulate through the basket.

2. Preheat the air fryer to 350 degrees.

3. In a bowl, soak the potatoes in the water for 1520 minutes, then drain in a colander and use some paper towel or clean cloth to pat dry.

4. In a large mixing bowl, shake the potato strips with the olive oil, salt, pepper, and bay seasoning. Ensure that all the potato strips are coated in oil and covered in seasonings on all sides.

5.   Arrange the potato strips in the air fryer basket.

6.   Set the air fryer timer to 20 minutes. Throughout the duration, vigorously shake the handle of the air fryer several times to jostle the potato strips and ensure a good even fry.

7.   After 20 minutes, when the air fryer shuts off, the potatoes should be perfectly golden crisped and the seasonings lightly toasted. Serve directly while hot!

NOTES:

There are almost as many preferred dipping sauces for bay seasoned fries as there are people who love them, so go with whatever you and your guests, family or friends prefer. I like my fries dipped in some nice fresh mayonnaise – just as they do in Belgium! And you can't go wrong with the old standby ketchup!

GARLIC CRISPY SWEET POTATO FRIES

Sweet potatoes are so healthy and an excellent source of Vitamin A, beta-carotene, and other important nutrients – and simply delectable when crispy fried and lightly seasoned. This dish is my go to recipe for the perfect side dish that's as wholesome as it is tasty. *(Recipe serves 2-3 people.)*

INGREDIENTS:

2 large or 3 medium sized sweet potatoes, washed, peeled, and sliced into strips approximately ½inch thick

3 cups of water

2 teaspoons of olive oil

½ teaspoon of garlic salt

Pinch of salt and pepper

½ teaspoon of paprika

INSTRUCTIONS:

1. Cover the basket of the air fryer with a lining of tin foil, leaving the edges uncovered to allow air to circulate through the basket.

2. Preheat the air fryer to 350 degrees.

3. In a bowl, soak the sweet potatoes in the water for 1520 minutes, then drain in a colander and use some paper towel or clean cloth to pat dry.

4. In a large mixing bowl, shake the sweet potato strips with the olive oil, salt, pepper, and bay seasoning. Ensure that all the sweet potato strips are coated in oil and covered in seasonings on all sides.

5. Place the sweet potato strips into the air fryer basket.

6. Set the air fryer timer to 20 minutes. Throughout the duration, vigorously shake the handle of the air fryer several times to jostle the sweet potato strips and ensure a good even fry.

7. After 20 minutes, when the air fryer shuts off, the sweet potatoes should be perfectly golden crisped and the seasonings lightly toasted. Serve directly while hot!

NOTES:

Ketchup is perfect with these sweet and crispy fries, or a little gravy from whatever meat dish you might be serving as the main course. Then again, with all the nutrients and flavor packed into these fries, I often just eat them as the main dish, maybe with a little protein on the side!

CRISPY FRIED BRUSSELS SPROUTS

You may not think of the ultra-nutritious Brussels sprout as a source of crispy, crunchy, savory deliciousness, but think again! This recipe uses only a tiny amount of oil and a pinch of salt, yet the sprouts come out perfect every time in the air fryer. *(Recipe serves 4-6 people.)*

INGREDIENTS:

1 cup of fresh or frozen Brussels sprouts, rinsed and patted dry, cut into quarters with the stems cut off

2 teaspoons of olive oil

Pinch of salt and pepper

OR PREHEAT TO 350° &
COOK 12 MIN

INSTRUCTIONS:

1. Cover the basket of the air fryer with a lining of tin foil, leaving the edges uncovered to allow air to circulate through the basket.

2. ~~Preheat the air fryer to 350 degrees.~~

3. In a bowl, toss the Brussels sprouts with the olive oil, salt and pepper.

4. Arrange the Brussels sprouts in a single layer on the lined air fryer basket.

5. Set the air fryer timer to 20 minutes. Throughout the duration, vigorously shake the handle of the air fryer several times to jostle the Brussels sprouts and ensure a good even fry.

6. After 20 minutes, when the air fryer shuts off, the sprouts will be perfectly cooked – crispy and browned on the outside, and juicy and nutritious on the inside. Serve directly while hot!

NOTES:

Believe it or not, kids will be pushing for their turn at a helping of these crunchy, salty bites of goodness. They wouldn't even believe you if you told them how extremely healthy they also are. So don't tell them, just enjoy watching children love their cruciferous veggies!

FRIED ZUCCHINI POPPERS

This is an old family favorite that I pull out every time there's a party, family gathering, or children's birthday party. These zucchini poppers are a wonderful way to get kids to eat their vegetables, as well as being a perfect cocktail snack for adults! *(Recipe serves 4-6 people.)*

INGREDIENTS:

2 medium sized zucchini, rinsed, patted dry, and sliced into bite sized pieces

1 tablespoon of grated or powdered Parmesan cheese

1 cup of breadcrumbs (Panko brand works well)

2 medium sized eggs

Pinch of salt and pepper

1 teaspoon of oregano

1 teaspoon of rosemary

INSTRUCTIONS:

1. Cover the basket of the air fryer with a lining of tin foil, leaving the edges uncovered to allow air to circulate through the basket.

2. Preheat the air fryer to 350 degrees.

3. In a mixing bowl, beat the eggs until fluffy and until the yolks and whites are fully combined, and set aside.

4. In a separate mixing bowl, combine the breadcrumbs, parmesan, oregano, rosemary, salt and pepper, and set aside.

5. Dip each piece of zucchini into the bowl with dry ingredients, coating all sides; then submerge into the bowl with wet ingredi-

ents, then dip again into the dry ingredients. This double coating will ensure an extra crisp and delicious air fry!

6. Lay the coated zucchini pieces on the foil covering the air fryer basket, in a single flat layer.

7. Set the air fryer timer for 10 minutes.

8. Shake the handle of the air fryer basket several times during cooking, to jostle the zucchini and ensure a good even fry.

9. After 10 minutes, the zucchini should be crispy, golden brown and perfect. Serve while hot!

NOTES:

I love a little ranch or bleu cheese dipping sauce with these, so if you have any serve some on the side for guests. These are an outstanding standalone snack, or a great side dish for any Italian themed meal. Have at 'em, and enjoy!

KICKIN' BUFFALO CAULIFLOWER

Calling all buffalo chicken lovers! This recipe makes it easy to enjoy buffalo flavor and keep things super healthy! With the flavor of the buffalo sauce shining through you won't even know you are eating cauliflower. What a healthy surprise! (Recipe serves 3-4 people.)

INGREDIENTS:

4 cups cauliflower, cut into bit sized pieces

1 tablespoon olive oil

2 teaspoons garlic powder

1/4 teaspoon salt

1/8 teaspoon pepper

1 tablespoon butter, melted

1/2 -3/4 cup Frank's Buffalo Wing Style hot sauce (use according to taste and desired heat level)

INSTRUCTIONS:

1. Cover the basket of the air fryer with a lining of tin foil, leaving the edges uncovered to allow air to circulate through the basket.

2. Preheat the air fryer to 390 degrees.

3. Use a gallon zip lock bag to help coat the cauliflower evenly. Add cauliflower and olive oil to the bag first and toss to coat.

4. Sprinkle in garlic powder, salt and pepper. Close zip lock and shake bag gently to disperse seasonings.

5. Pour seasoned cauliflower into the air fryer basket and set timer for 6 minutes.

6.   Meanwhile, stir together melted butter and Buffalo hot sauce in a small bowl.

7.   When air fryer shuts off, cauliflower should just be getting crispy. Remove from the air fryer using tongs – careful not to burn your fingers! Place cauliflower in a large bowl and pour the hot sauce mixture over top. Stir gently to cover all the pieces of cauliflower.

8.   Return to the air fryer at 320 degrees for 5 minutes.

9.   When the timer goes off and the air fryer shuts off, remove the cauliflower from the basket carefully. Serve hot with your favorite dipping sauce.

NOTES:

Paired with carrots, celery and a little dipping sauce, this really is the ultimate appetizer for the health conscious. The air fryer even manages to give the cauliflower a little crunch so you don't feel like you are missing out.

ITALIAN MUSHROOMS

The perfect accompaniment to a steak dinner, these mushrooms are incredibly easy and can elevate any meal to restaurant quality. Mushroom lovers will delight in the simple flavors that really allow the mushrooms to shine, while bringing great flavor to the dish. Next time you are grilling steaks, I encourage you to pair them with these mushrooms. You'll be glad you did! (Recipe serves 4 people.)

INGREDIENTS:

2 pounds mushrooms, gently washed and dried then cut into quarters

2-3 tablespoons olive oil

1/2 teaspoon garlic powder

2 teaspoons Italian Herb Seasoning

2 tablespoons dry white wine

INSTRUCTIONS:

1. Cover the basket of the air fryer with a lining of tin foil, leaving the edges uncovered to allow air to circulate through the basket.

2. Preheat the air fryer to 320 degrees.

3. In a small bowl, whisk together the olive oil, garlic powder, Italian Herbs and the white wine. With mushrooms in a large bowl, pour the olive oil mixture over top of the mushrooms and toss gently until all mushrooms are well coated.

4. Place the mushrooms on the foil in the air fryer basket and set the timer for 25 minutes.

5.   Halfway through the cooking open up the drawer and give the mushrooms a good stir to insure even cooking.

6.   After 25 minutes, when the air fryer shuts off, open the drawer and carefully scoop the mushrooms into a bowl using a spoon. Serve hot.

NOTES:

Though many would consider these mushrooms to be the perfect side dish, I've found that they really have many uses. With a ranch or marinara dip, these mushrooms make a simple, but yummy appetizer. They are also a heavenly topping on a baked potato or even spaghetti.

5

DESSERTS

CREAMY CRUSTY CHEESECAKE

One bite into this classic New York style cheesecake, and you'll be smitten. The creamy sweet filling and crumbly graham cracker crust pretty much guarantee love at first taste. This is the sort of high end dessert that can cost a pretty penny when ordered in a restaurant or a grocery store. Now you can make it perfectly right in your own home with no muss, no fuss, and all the flavor! *(Recipe serves 4-6 people.)*

INGREDIENTS:

16 ounces of softened room temperature cream cheese

1 teaspoon of vanilla extract

1 tablespoon of brown sugar

1 teaspoon of ground cinnamon

1 medium sized egg

1 cup of sweetened condensed milk

1 cup of crumbled graham cracker crumbs

2 tablespoons of white sugar

1 small pat of butter (melted)

INSTRUCTIONS:

1. Preheat the air fryer to 350 degrees.

2. Lightly grease a 6-inch spring form pan.

3. Using a blender or a food processor, grind the graham cracker crumbs finely, then pour them in a large mixing bowl and stir in the white sugar and pat of butter (melted).

4. Pour the graham cracker mixture into the greased pan, and press around the edges to flatten it against the dish.

5. Place the pan with crust into the air fryer basket, and set timer for 5 minutes.

6. After 5 minutes, remove the pan with crust using tongs or oven mitts, and set aside to cool.

7. In the large mixing bowl, combine the cream cheese, vanilla extract, brown sugar, cinnamon, condensed milk and the egg. Whip thoroughly, so that all the ingredients are thoroughly mixed, thick and fluffy and slightly stiff.

8. Pour the wet mixture into the pan with the graham cracker crust, and smooth out the top with a butter knife or spatula. Set the pan inside the lined air fry basket.

9. Reset the air fryer to 350 degrees for 40 minutes.

10. After 40 minutes, remove the pan with oven mitts. Allow to cool on the counter before placing in the fridge for an hour to chill before serving.

NOTES:

This creamy, luscious dessert goes great with some fresh berries if you have them, or jam if fresh fruit is hard to find. This dessert is absolute melt in your mouth magic, so serve it up often!

RASPBERRY CREAM ROLL UPS

This recipe offers a delightful sweetened variation of crispy delicious spring rolls. Instead of poultry or vegetables filling, these awesome dessert finger food snacks pack a dollop of sweet cream cheese filling and fresh raspberries. They're a dessert built to share, though make sure you make enough for everyone to get the second helping they'll crave! *(Recipe serves 3-4 people.)*

INGREDIENTS:

1 cup of fresh raspberries, rinsed and patted dry

½ cup of cream cheese, softened to room temperature

¼ cup of brown sugar

¼ cup of sweetened condensed milk

1 egg

1 teaspoon of corn starch

6 spring roll wrappers (any brand will do, I like Blue Dragon or Tasty Joy, both available through Target or Walmart, or any large grocery chain)

¼ cup of water, for sealing

INSTRUCTIONS:

1. Cover the basket of the air fryer with a lining of tin foil, leaving a ½inch uncovered at the edges to allow air to circulate.

2. Preheat the air fryer to 350 degrees.

3. In a mixing bowl, combine the cream cheese, brown sugar, condensed milk, cornstarch, and egg. Beat or whip thoroughly, until all ingredients are completely mixed and fluffy, thick and stiff.

4. Spoon even amounts of the creamy filling into each spring roll wrapper, then top each dollop of filling with several raspberries.

5. Roll up the wraps around the creamy raspberry filling, and seal the seams with a few dabs of water.

6. Place each roll on the foil lined air fryer basket, seams facing down.

7. Set the air fryer timer to 10 minutes. During cooking, shake the handle of the fryer basket to ensure a nice even surface crisp.

8. After 10 minutes, when the air fryer shuts off, the spring rolls should be golden brown and perfect on the outside, while the raspberries and cream filling will have cooked together in a glorious fusion. Remove with tongs and serve hot or cold.

NOTES:

This is the kind of simple yet elegant dessert that makes everyone feel fancy. These sweet rolls go terrific with afternoon coffee or tea, or as a sweet treat before bedtime. Enjoy!

GOOEY CHEWY CHOCOLATE BROWNIES

Well, here it is folks – the mother of all desserts, the standard by which your entire dessert repertoire will be judged. Thank heavens, this awesome brownie recipe is so simple and absolutely delicious. The brownies come out moist and rich every time, and they could not be easier. *(Recipe serves 4-6 people.)*

INGREDIENTS:

½ cup of unsalted butter, melted

1 small pat of butter for greasing the pan

1 cup of white sugar

1 teaspoon of vanilla extract

2 eggs

½ cup of all-purpose flour

1/3 cup of unsweetened chocolate cocoa powder

¼ teaspoon of baking powder

Pinch of salt

INSTRUCTIONS:

1. Preheat the air fryer to 350 degrees.

2. Lightly grease a 6-inch heat safe metal or ceramic baking pan with the pat of butter.

3. In a medium sized mixing bowl, stir together the melted butter, eggs, and vanilla extract; beat or whip thoroughly until slightly fluffy and all ingredients are thoroughly combined.

4. In a larger, separate mixing bowl, combine the flour, sugar, cocoa, salt, and baking powder.

5. Slowly and steadily pour the dry ingredients into the wet ingredients, stirring continuously until thoroughly blended and until there are no lumps in the batter.

6. Pour the batter into the cake pan, leaving at least a ¼ inch space at the top to allow for the brownies to rise.

7. Set the pan in the air fryer basket, and set the air fryer timer to 20 minutes.

8. After 20 minutes, when the air fryer shuts off, test the brownies with a toothpick or a knife. If it comes out clean, they're done! If there is still some wet batter, reset the timer for another few minutes.

9. When ready, remove the pan with oven mitts and set to cool for several minutes before cutting and serving.

NOTES:

This is such a heavenly treat all on its own, though if you want to take it to the next level, serve with a dollop of whipped cream or a scoop of vanilla ice cream. Any way you accessorize them, these brownies are a wonderful sweet chocolate treat.

CRISPY APPLE CRUMBLE

This dish is not only one of the greatest desserts of all time, it's also the ultimate sweet tooth comfort food. There's nothing quite so soothing as hot, tart apples simmered in brown sugar and cinnamon, topped with a perfect crispy crumbly topping. This is my family's go to dessert for cold winter nights, and I know you'll love it too! *(Recipe serves 3-4 people.)*

INGREDIENTS:

5 medium sized green or red apples – pick a brand with a good balance of sweetness to tartness – peeled and diced into small chunks

1 cup of brown sugar

1 teaspoon of cinnamon

1 medium sized lemon

½ cup of unsalted butter

1 cup of all-purpose flour

INSTRUCTIONS:

1. Preheat the air fryer to 3-40 degrees.

2. Lightly grease a 6-inch heat safe metal or ceramic baking pan with the pat of butter.

3. In a mixing bowl, combine the apple chunks, the juice from the lemon, and half the butter, half the brown sugar, and half the cinnamon. Combine thoroughly until the ingredients are thoroughly mixed.

4. In a separate mixing bowl, combine the remainder of the butter, brown sugar, and cinnamon, until it forms a crumbly consistency.

5.   Pour the apple mixture into the greased baking pan, and spread it evenly in the pan.

6.   Spread the crumbly sugar cinnamon and butter mixture over the apple mixture in the pan, spreading evenly but allowing chunks to remain.

7.   Set the air fryer timer to 10 minutes, and place the pan on the surface of the air fryer.

8.   After 10 minutes, when the air fryer shuts off, remove using oven mitts and serve cool or hot.

NOTES:

This dessert is the epitome of sweet comfort, and it'll keep just fine for a few days. For an extra dose of goodness, serve with some fresh cream or ice cream. This may not be the healthiest way to get a serving of apples, but it is one of the most delicious.

CHOCOLATE CHIP CUPCAKES

What's better than cake for dessert? Why, multiple little cakes that everyone can hold in their hands, of course! Children and adults alike will be delighted with this recipe for chocolate chip cupcakes, which will bring out everyone's sweet tooth for a treat. *(Recipe serves 1-2 people.)*

INGREDIENTS:

½ cup of white sugar

1 ½ cups of all-purpose flour

2 teaspoons of baking powder

½ teaspoon of salt

2/3 cup of vegetable oil

1 medium sized egg

2 teaspoons of vanilla extract

1/4 cup vanilla yogurt

1 cup of chocolate chips

INSTRUCTIONS:

1. In a large bowl, mix the sugar, flour, baking powder and salt. Stir well to ensure all the dry ingredients are combined evenly.

2. In a separate, smaller bowl, pour oil, then add egg, yogurt, and vanilla extract. Whisk or beat thoroughly, until ingredients are uniformly combined and slightly fluffy.

3. Pour the wet mixture into the larger bowl with the dry ingredients, and combine evenly with a fork or handheld whisk. (Do *not*

use an electric beater – you do not want to overmix the batter, or the cupcakes will come out chewy and dense!)

4.   Add the chocolate chips, and gently fold in with a spatula or wooden spoon.

5.   Place silicone cupcake baking cups in the air fryer basket. The basket should fit four or five cupcake cups comfortably – better to do two batches than to overcrowd!

6.   Spoon batter into each of the cupcake cups, filling them up about ¾ of the way.

7.   Set the air fryer to 350 degrees for 10 minutes.

8.   After 10 minutes, the air fryer will shut off. Remove the basket and test cupcakes by sticking a toothpick inside – if the toothpick comes out dry, your cupcakes are ready! If not, reset the air fryer to 320 degrees for 2 minutes, or until the toothpick comes out dry.

9.   Remove your finished cupcakes from the frying basket and set aside to cool. Place more cupcake cups on the baking tray, and repeat until all your batter is used up (this recipe should make 11 or 1-2 cupcakes). Serve hot or cold.

NOTES:

A dab of chocolate spread such as Nutella goes great with these as a makeshift frosting, though really the cupcakes are moist and chocolatey enough on their own not to need anything. Kids especially love these tasty treats. There's no fork required! Enjoy and share with everyone.

CARAMEL WALNUT BLONDIES

This crunchy, gooey, yummy dessert is such a great treat to serve at a party. I love the combination of caramel and walnuts together, with the moist vanilla goodness of these perfect blondies. These are the ideal choice when you want a dessert that's both unexpected and delightful. *(Recipe serves 3-4 people.)*

INGREDIENTS:

½ cup of unsalted butter

1 small pat of butter for greasing the pan

1 cup of white sugar

1 teaspoon of vanilla extract

2 eggs

½ cup of all-purpose flour

1/3 cup of walnuts, shelled and coarsely ground

½ cup of caramel chips

¼ teaspoon of baking powder

Pinch of salt

INSTRUCTIONS:

1. Preheat the air fryer to 3-40 degrees.

2. Lightly grease a 6-inch heat safe metal or ceramic baking pan with the pat of butter.

3. In a medium sized mixing bowl, stir together the melted butter, eggs, and vanilla extract. Beat or whip thoroughly until slightly fluffy and all ingredients are thoroughly combined.

4. In a larger, separate mixing bowl, combine the flour, sugar, walnuts, caramel chips, salt, and baking powder.

5. Slowly and steadily pour the dry ingredients into the wet ingredients, stirring continuously and until thoroughly blended and until there are no lumps in the batter.

6. Pour the batter into the cake pan, leaving at least a ¼ inch space at the top to allow for the brownies to rise.

7. Set the pan in the lined air fryer basket, and set the air fryer timer to 20 minutes.

8. After 20 minutes, when the air fryer shuts off, test the blondies with a toothpick or a knife – if it comes out clean, they're done! If there is still some wet batter, reset the timer for another few minutes.

9. When ready, remove the pan with oven mitts and set to cool for several minutes before cutting and serving.

NOTES:

A little ice cream or whipped cream pairs perfectly with these, or even a drizzle of chocolate or caramel syrup. If you're baking for those with nut allergies, it's easy to just cut the walnuts from the recipe and keep the other ingredients the same. Everyone will love these treats, so get ready to share – just save one or two for yourself, of course!

CHOCOLATE CREAM PIE

This awesome and easy recipe for chocolate cream pie is absolutely ir-resistible. The graham cracker crust is a particularly decadent touch, and goes perfectly with the rich chocolate goodness. Go ahead and pinch yourself – this chocolate cream pie is no dream! *(Recipe serves 3-4 people.)*

INGREDIENTS:

1 cup of unsweetened dark cocoa powder

16 ounces of softened room temperature cream cheese

½ cup of white sugar

1 teaspoon of vanilla extract

1 teaspoon of ground cinnamon

1 medium sized egg

1 cup of sweetened condensed milk

1 cup of crumbled graham cracker crumbs

2 tablespoons of brown sugar

1 small pat of butter, melted

INSTRUCTIONS:

1. Preheat the air fryer to 350 degrees.

2. Lightly grease a 6-inch pie pan.

3. Using a blender or a food processor, grind the graham cracker crumbs finely, then pour them in a large mixing bowl and stir in the brown sugar and melted butter.

4. Pour the graham cracker mixture into the greased pie pan, and press around the edges to flatten it against the dish.

5. Place the pan with crust into the air fryer basket, and set timer for 5 minutes.

6. After 5 minutes, remove the pan with crust using tongs or oven mitts, and set aside to cool.

7. In the large mixing bowl, combine the cocoa powder, cream cheese, vanilla extract, white sugar, cinnamon, condensed milk and the egg. Whip thoroughly, so that all the ingredients are thoroughly mixed, thick, fluffy and slightly stiff.

8. Pour the wet chocolatey mixture into the pan with the graham cracker crust, and smooth out the top with a butter knife or spatula. Set the pan inside the air fry basket.

9. Reset the air fryer to 350 degrees for 40 minutes.

10. After 40 minutes, remove the pan with oven mitts, cool on the counter before placing in the fridge for an hour to chill before serving.

NOTES:

This delectable dessert goes perfectly with some fresh whipped cream, ice cream, or even a side of strawberries. Of course, it's also a total taste sensation all on its own, so don't feel the need to serve with anything – except a smile, and a readiness to have your friends, family and guests wowed by your cooking prowess!

CINNAMON SUGAR DONUTS

Who doesn't love a gooey, sugary donut? Especially when warm, the fried dough practically melts in your mouth. The taste is sensational... but my waistline usually disagrees. Thanks to the air fryer, and a simple baking trick, you can enjoy donuts that are at least a little healthier and we think that's a good thing! (Serves 8 people.)

INGREDIENTS:

1 can of large buttermilk biscuits (not the flaky kind)

1 teaspoon cinnamon

1/4 cup sugar

INSTRUCTIONS:

1. Preheat the air fryer to 300 degrees.

2. Open the canned biscuits and separate the individual biscuits. Lay on parchment paper or a clean counter.

3. Using a 1 to 1 1/2 inch round cookie cutter or similar sized round object, cut the middle hole from each biscuit so it then resembles a donut. Don't discard the small circle! These make perfect donut holes!

4. Place about 4 donuts into the air fryer basket, so the donuts are not touching. Set the air fryer timer for 5 minutes. While donuts are cooking, use a shallow bowl and mix together the cinnamon and sugar.

5. After 5 minutes, when the air fryer shuts off, carefully remove the donuts from the basket using tongs. Repeat cooking process with remaining donuts.

6. When donuts are pulled from the air fryer and still warm, dip them in the cinnamon sugar mixture, being sure to coat all sides. Serve warm, or cooled if you want to wait that long!

NOTES:

Experiment with your favorite donut toppings by mixing together a simple icing, adding sprinkles or even drizzling with melted chocolate. These little treats go great with a cup of hot coffee or tea and they are the perfect size for dunking.

Made in the USA
Middletown, DE
06 December 2023